Verge 2016

Verge 2016

Futures

Edited by Megan Blake, Annie Bourke
and Bonnie Reid

MONASH University
Publishing

Monash University Publishing
Matheson Library and Information Services Building
40 Exhibition Walk
Monash University
Clayton, Victoria 3800, Australia
www.publishing.monash.edu

Monash University Publishing brings to the world publications which advance the best traditions of humane and enlightened thought.

Monash University Publishing titles pass through a rigorous process of independent peer review.

www.publishing.monash.edu/books/verge2016-9781925495065.html

Series: Verge

Design: Les Thomas

Cover image: © 2016 Jesse Boyd-Reid

National Library of Australia Cataloguing-in-Publication entry:

Title:	Verge 2016 : futures / edited by Megan Blake, Annie Bourke, Bonnie Reid.
ISBN:	9781925495065 (paperback)
Subjects:	Creative writing--Fiction.
	Short stories, Australian.
	Short stories, English.
	Poetry--21st century
	Poetry, Modern--21st century
Other Creators/Contributors:	
	Blake, Megan, editor.
	Bourke, Annie, editor.
	Reid, Bonnie, editor.
Dewey number:	A823.0108

Printed in Australia by Griffin Press an Accredited ISO AS/NZS 14001:2004 Environmental Management System printer.

The paper this book is printed on is certified against the Forest Stewardship Council ® Standards. Griffin Press holds FSC chain of custody certification SGS-COC-005088. FSC promotes environmentally responsible, socially beneficial and economically viable management of the world's forests.

Contents

TEXTUAL COMPOSITIONS

VISUAL COMPOSITION

CONTRIBUTORS

Foreword

The theme of this year's edition of *Verge* was born from a discussion on the present: on concerns we had about the world as it stood; on emerging movements and conversations that encouraged and inspired us; on the diverse threads of belief and practice and ideology that didn't necessarily resolve themselves into one coherent image of 'current society'. There was minimal brainstorming involved in the decision: we wanted this edition to be political. And what we saw all around us in Australian politics was a deep rift between government policy and the needs and wants of this country's growing and diversifying population. This is not a new state of play for Australia. But events in recent years such as the continued refusal of a treaty acknowledging the sovereignty of Indigenous Australians, the turning around of asylum seeker boats, the severe cuts to funding of the Arts and to the Safe Schools program, the corporatisation of tertiary education, and the unconscionable government response to the climate change crisis we are facing leaves us all with the burning question: What is the future of this country; and, equally importantly, the future of the world at large?

Time flows in the small universe of conversation the same as it does in the ages of the universe measured in years, millennia, so it is not surprising that a conversation that began focused on the present moved to the past and the future; and, a theme that began in the present evolved into the tracing of a path that connected the *now*, as a product of the *then*, with the unknown multiplicities of what *will be*. We wanted the 2016 edition of *Verge* to be a similar conversation, where our contributors could express their experiences of despair, their rage at past and ongoing injustices, their ideas for change, and their hopes for better, brighter and more inclusive futures.

Writing has the power to exalt, to enlighten, to animate, to confuse, to enrage, to gratify, to relieve, to grieve, to hope. In the pages that follow we have collected together an exciting new selection of fiction, non-fiction, poetry, and visual essay from emerging and established writers that exemplifies all these qualities – with some authors speaking expressly on historical and contemporary issues including the Nauru 'solution', the devastation of the natural environment and ecosystems, and the sexual abuse perpetrated by clergy; with others questioning more deep-rooted and systemic issues such as the social significance of race, of gender, and the hypocrisy and double-standards of privilege, that see themselves manifested over and over in diverse places and times; and still others reflecting on the cycle of causation and change that is contained in the idea of the future, the cycle of past–present–future, and to what extent we can ever escape – deviate – start fresh.

From amongst the collection we are very pleased to have chosen the winning and runner-up pieces for the *Verge* Prizes for Fiction and Poetry, and to publish both the 2016 winner of the prestigious Monash Prize for literature and the highest-placing piece from a Monash University student. The winner of the *Verge* Prize for Poetry is 'Bellyache' by Callum Methven, with which we are happy to open our collection, and the runner-up is 'the sound of a new body' by Chi Tran. We hope that 'Bellyache' triggers the same bittersweet heart-pain as it did for us, and that 'the sound of a new body' gives you a similar sense of place to cling to in a perversely ambivalent no-place. The winner of the *Verge* Prize for Fiction is 'While these Palm Trees Sleep' by Jamie Marina Lau, and the runner-up is 'The Ugly Son' by Alice Whitmore. We hope you enjoy the creativity of form displayed by both writers, and are able to use the style to enter into the lives and minds of the narrators, even – in a radically phenomenological turn – more fully than they are able to themselves. It is difficult enough to create either a sophisticated discourse or a fully-realised psyche; to do both is rare. The Monash Prize is awarded for the best short story submitted by a student of any Australian or New Zealand university, and *Verge* is pleased to partner with the Emerging Writers Festival in the publication of the winner. This year 'Ghost Story' by Phoebe Chen was selected by the judges, and we consider ourselves lucky to have the opportunity to feature it in this collection, beautifully quirky and evocative – realistic when it needs to be and whimsically Kafkaesque when it does not – as it is. The highest-placing piece from a Monash University student is 'The Beggar and the Glimpse', by Calvin Fung, with its transportation of the reader to current-day Hong Kong.

We hope that you enjoy being taken on a journey along these paths through the past, the present and the future, and, whether some pieces evoke an immediate response or others sit with you for longer, that you consider the whole of this collection at the end of the day, as we do, a happily good read.

Acknowledgments

The editors of Verge would like to acknowledge that this publication was produced on stolen land of the Kulin nations, and we pay our respect to Elders past and present, with gratitude that we were able to collect and share these stories there.

Many thanks for their time and assistance in directly making this publication possible is extended appreciatively to:

Dr Ali Alizadeh, *Verge* Coordinator
Dr Melinda Harvey, Melbourne Writers Festival and Emerging Writers Festival Liaison
Assoc Prof Kevin Foster, Director of the Literary and Cultural Studies Graduate Program
Dr Nathan Hollier and Joanne Mullins, Melbourne University Publishing
Kylie Maslen, Melbourne Writers Festival
Kate Callingham, Emerging Writers Festival
Evie Kendal, Editor of *Colloquy*
Yasmin Chilmeran and Nicholas Sofos, Monash University
Sally Riley and Jocelyne Mohamudally, Monash University

Gratitude for the time and effort donated, so that pieces could be critically reviewed with expertise and a generous reading, goes to:

Dr Ali Alizadeh
Dr Benjamin Andreo
Associate Professor Craig Batty
Dr Glenn D'Cruz
Dr Sally Gardner
Dr Meghan Kelly
Dr Alyson Miller
Associate Professor Jane Montgomery Griffiths
Dr Gabriel Garcia-Ochoa
Dr Emily Potter
Dr Patrizia Sambuco
Dr Ann Vickery

Dr Chris Watkin
Dr Christiane Weller

We and the contributors thank you for your valuable feedback.

Special thanks for support and other forms of assistance too numerous and diverse to name:

Mike Blackney
Grady Bourke
Kitlyn Bourke
Clancy Reid
Phoebe Reid

And, finally:

The contributors. We are proud to work on something with you that champions the creative arts, original expression, public discourse and the arts as a respected profession. Thank you for your industry and imagination in developing these pieces; may you always have money and a room of your own in which to do it.

1

Bellyache

Callum Methven

WINNER OF THE VERGE PRIZE FOR POETRY

My memories are fading brown like old photographs like that one hanging on
Your wall in the entry that we took down at the Church of St
Mary and Henry's wedding what a lovely couple
How you loved the cheesecake how you loved the bellyache of
Aunt Tessa's terrible jokes almost made me cry but you never did
Never even blinked never even stopped wondering if this was all there was

Youth was an easier game so young so young just a girl an only
Child and every Sunday afternoon mother went to visit her friend left you alone
So you climbed up the withered bones of the ancient ghost gum with the
Waves of the bush lapping at your feet vertigo whispering in your ear don't
Fall don't fall and the kookaburra laughed so shrill but you didn't get it

Just last night you saw a blinking light in the sky in the tight gulf between two
horizons and
Michael said it was an angel and you chided him a blinking
Angel spinning around a world so flat one might slide her under the door I hope
To look as good at six millennia little one when did you become so naïve
And I so cynical

He wrote a letter young boy only child had to trace his name letter to the editor
said
Please send me to the reef where I belong please can you
Send me to the reef it won't be here for long because the bell is ringing
Church bells ringing hats on kids it's hot outside

Grey sky grey house grey hair on my head is falling out like you fell out of the
tree so
Old we have become not even our photographs are safe from the present
Please send me back to where I once belonged back
To the church that day before the future ruined it for us and
Everyone else and mother and Michael if you'll just let us write you a letter
Or better,
Go back to ghosts of us
Back to the ghost gum tree with me and we can live and be free again
Just you and me again
Kookaburra laughs so shrill so shall we when I tell you
The end of the joke

2

Harmond Drive

Cecilia Harris

It took Mike five minutes to assure himself that the dog we hit on Harmond Drive was dead. The border collie had emerged from the side of the six lane highway. Mike slammed on the brakes but we hit it straight on as it cowered, bracing itself for the impact. Pasta salad flung from the bowl on the backseat, spraying the windscreen. The inertia whacked us back into our seats. We sat waiting for something – anything – to happen. The dog was dead, surely. It was dead and I had never seen a person so unsure of something so finished as Mike was about that dog.

Mike nudged it with his foot, stared at it, talked at it like a child. I stood watching from behind the opened passenger door. Its fur rippled in the wind, as if its spirit were fighting the end. I think Mike might have stopped trying a little earlier if it weren't for the wind.

'What'll we do, Sal?' Mike looked at me, his face tormented.

'Check the collar,' I said. Mike groped around its neck.

'Nah. God. He's still warm. Who owns a border collie and doesn't put a collar on it?'

'Might be a stray,' but the clean sheen of the dog's soft coat implied otherwise.

We took a picnic blanket from the back of the '91 Mitsubishi Lancer and splayed it out on the side of the road. It was understood, without saying, that we would both be lifting the dog onto the blanket. We would both be taking responsibility for this. Mike waited for me to close the boot.

'You ready?' I had never seen him this disappointed. We had known each other for three whole years, but I could never have imagined that face.

I took the initiative, grabbing the dog's back legs. Mike followed straight after with the front. We lifted it, just enough not to drag the body, and shuffled across to the blanket.

'Shit!' Mike yelled, dropping his end of the corpse.

'Did you feel that?'

'What?'

'He moved, I swear he fucken moved.' Mike stood, arms out, ready to tackle the dog in an instant.

'Mike. He's dead. I'm sorry, but —'

'Look! Fucken look at him!'

I looked down at the animal. It lay there, still as ever, its clean fur dancing horribly in the wind. Dead. Blood had started to appear around its mouth.

'For fuck sake. It's dead. Stop. You're freaking me out.'

'I could have sworn it moved.'

We wrapped the dog in the blanket and carried it to the car. We covered the spilt pasta salad with newspaper and Mike put the dog on the back seat. I wiped down the inside of the windscreen while Mike smoked a cigarette.

We got back into the car and sat in silence.

'To the vet? You take dead animals to the vet, don't ya?' Mike lit another cigarette.

He didn't seem ready to start the car.

'I can drive. You call Marie and let her know we'll be late.'

'What's it fucken matter. She doesn't want us there anyway.'

It was Mike's daughter's sixth birthday. Marie was Georgia's mother. Once I'd got myself involved with Mike, the situation was as good as my problem.

'Georgia's your girl too.'

'What do you care?'

'She's your daughter, Mike. And I'm not gonna get around with a dickhead who doesn't turn up to his daughter's birthday party.' I got out of the car and walked around to the driver's side door. The only way to get Mike out of a rut was to drag him out headfirst. I stood and waited for him to decide whether or not he was going to let me drive. A patch of black fur lodged on the headlight whispered about. Mike sighed and moved to get out, stopping to look up at me. We really hit that dog hard.

'Thanks, Sal.'

Mike walked around the front of the car, stopping to look at the ground.

'Jesus. We really smacked him.'

✳

I was surprised by Marie. She was entirely likeable. I expected someone prickly, stubborn. From what Mike had said, I expected a woman uptight and tired, and I was expecting her to hate me.

Marie opened the door, beaming a warm smile from behind the flywire. Greeting us with a sing-song hello, hugging and kissing us both, she welcomed us inside. Marie was beautiful. And not just the pretty kind. Marie was the full-throttle, born in a bath of grace and purity kind of beautiful.

'It is so great to finally meet you, Sal,' Marie whispered to me, ushering me into the corner of the room. 'I'm worried about Mike. But he told me about you, and I have to say I felt really relieved.'

'I dunno about that.' I laughed. It was more of a chuckle. How do I not look foolish in front of this incredible woman?

'No really. His last two girlfriends, you know, they were nice. But Mike needs a certain type of partner, I think. He gets, you know —'

'Down,' we whispered in unison.

'Yes. See? You get that. The others didn't get that. Not as far as I could tell. The last one, Sandra —'

'Amanda,' I corrected.

'Amanda. Amanda coddled him. And, you know —'

Georgia ran in from the backyard, five screaming children in tow. She ran straight to Marie and stopped, panting, waiting for her turn to speak.

'Yes, Georgia?'

'Can-we-go-out-front-and-play-tips?'

'Yes but you'll need to take Dad out there with you, to keep an eye out for cars.' Marie gestured her head over to Mike with a smile.

'Hi Georgie. Happy birthday,' Mike said. He had done worse. Mike and children were a difficult combination. I'd often thought it felt cruel just how uncomfortable he was around kids, and then, you know, Georgia happening.

'Go give Dad a kiss and hug, please Georgia.' Marie nudged her gently in Mike's direction. Walking over to him bashfully, looking back at her mother, the little girl kissed him gingerly on the cheek. Georgia patted his arm in the way children do of a dog they're not quite sure of. Or was it more with the reverence required of touching the nose of a horse. I couldn't tell.

'What's that?' Georgia grimaced, pointing at Mike's ear.

'What's what?' He pulled away from her, raising a hand to the side of his head.

'Gross,' Georgia groaned. I smiled. Georgia appeared to be more like the Marie Mike had told me about than Marie herself. 'Mike has pasta in his ear.'

'Oh,' I intersected. 'We had a pasta salad on the backseat of the car on the way over, and —' I was unsure if I should tell them, but I saw no other way of explaining it, 'and we hit a dog. The pasta went everywhere.'

'Oh my god. Are you guys okay?' Marie looked genuinely concerned. I am sure she *was* genuinely concerned.

'Yeah, we're fine. Mike's a bit shaken up. But he'll be fine, I think.'

News of the accident floated through Georgia without record. She ran back to the yard, making up a song about Mike, pasta and hairy ears. The other children joined in.

'Who invited that guy,' Mike asked Marie. He was referring to a tall, sallow man standing at the other end of the room. The man stood alone among the other parents, vacantly picking at his teeth.

'I did, Mike. Sal, that's Georgia's after-school care supervisor.'

'He's a fucken weirdo,' Mike said.

'He is not.'

'He can't hold a conversation without flaring his nostrils,' Mike said.

'Wayne, honey, come meet Sal,' Marie chirped across the room. Mike had registered the word 'honey' as soon as I had. Wayne grinned and waddled across the room. Marie took him by the hand.

'Hullo.' Wayne offered me a handshake.

'Sal,' I said.

'Wayne,' he replied, nostrils quivering.

'Sal is Mike's new partner.' Marie smiled at me sincerely.

'Looks like you have a new partner too,' Mike interjected.

'Well,' Wayne smirked, 'we are taking everything very slow. You know, just seeing how things go.' He had a lisp.

'Right. Yep. So, do you guys make out behind the sports shed at school?'

'Mike,' Marie warned.

'No, really. Wouldn't want to let the kids see it, hey Wayne?'

'Mike.'

'Actually, Mike, Marie and I have decided that we are strictly platonic around the kids at school. We think it's best that way to begin with.'

'What? Like all the kids running around the house right now?'

'Mike, would you stop it please?'

'Come on, let's go sit out front.' I led him off. Wayne was a deer in headlights.

We grabbed a couple of beers and sat on the front step, watching the kids run around. Mike was noticeably annoyed. It hadn't occurred to him that his anger regarding Marie's love life might offend me.

'What a fucken dick,' Mike sneered. 'I mean, of all the men in this town,' he continued, 'and she chooses him?'

'Maybe he chose her,' I said.

'Yeah. Right,' he said, a spiteful smile building itself up across his face. 'Guys like that don't choose women like Marie. Marie does the choosing. Trust me.'

'Did she choose you?'

'What's that supposed to mean?'

'I guess I just don't see why Wayne was such a bad choice.'

'You're kidding.'

'You're always so pissed with Marie. She's nice. I like her. And you need to hate her.'

Mike said nothing. I left him on the step and headed for the train station. He spoke when I needed silence, and said nothing when I wanted him to explain everything.

I stayed at Mum's place that night. We sat up till 2:30am drinking whisky and hot water.

'Is it about kids? Cause if it's about kids, Sal, well, you're still young.'

'It's not about kids.'

'Then what's your problem? Ditch him. You're still young.'

'Mum.'

'Okay, love. Look. The way I see it,' she paused to light another cigarette, 'the way I see it is this. You've got your main roads, your proper arteries. They're the solid ones. Easy moving, you know? Then you've got your minor roads, the ones that take you sideways.'

'Mike's a road now?'

'Well,' she tilted her head, blowing the smoke sideways. 'Yes, but not a main artery.'

'My life isn't a metaphor.'

'Just cause Mike's a minor road, doesn't mean you shouldn't give it a shot. I just mean that, you know, he might be worthy of your time and energy Sal, but, maybe just to lead you someplace else.'

I poured another whisky.

'You do what you like. But believe me, you're young. You've got nothing to worry about.'

The evening went on like that until Mum got too drunk to sit upright. I put her to bed and set up the fold-out bed in the living room.

I lay awake listening to her snore. My father had never been Mum's main road. That had always been clear.

The next day I borrowed Mum's car and drove over to Mike's place. I let myself in and found him sitting on the deck chair in the overgrown yard. He didn't notice me at first. He sat still, the sun lighting the bugs and dust that floated around him. He lifted the tinny to his mouth and swigged. It was 11:30am.

'Sal,' he said.

'Mike,' I replied.

'Where'd you get off to?'

'Stayed at Mum's.'

'You got the shits?'

'No.'

'Righto then.'

'How was the rest of the party?' I sat on the side of the deck chair, taking a sidelong glance at his face. It was calm.

'I called the vet. No one claimed the dog.' He finished his beer in one mouthful, crushed the can and tossed it into the overgrown lawn. A stir of bugs spiralled skyward.

A child squealed in the park across the road. The toddler was defiantly upset. Had he climbed all that way to the top of the play equipment, had he made all that progress, just to be forced to go down the slide? Forced by way of gravity, and in the face of pure fear, to move into the future that awaited him below. His mother stood at the base of the slide, imploring his courage. How could he possibly turn back?

'Thought maybe we might get a dog, when you move your gear in next month.'

'We haven't decided that yet.'

'You're here all the time. Makes sense.' He shrugged.

He still hadn't looked at me. It was clear now that he never would.

'I can't stop thinking about that dog.'

3

Orange Gardens

Gavin Yates

Convulsive, the hammers of a piano…
Argentina stripped   & wandering houses
bathing in the reeds. Fractured images of displaced

lips still

as they are pinched,
stitched with the alphabet.   The lantana drinks from her mother's perfume…
shaking into dark   moderate.

In the orange gardens of the moon
always dreamt of
I often find myself…

a shell closing on elephantine
chords. Slow,

with conviction   & rigorous sadness.

4

Ghost Story

Phoebe Chen

WINNER OF THE MONASH PRIZE

The translator in the room across the hallway spoke five languages and was here to lose one of them. We met him on the way back from breakfast, teeth turmeric-stained, wrists bandaged up to his elbows. His room had a balcony that overlooked the clearing, ocean lapping at the mountains. Light piled onto water, unknowably bright. The greens here were really something, hidden in thickets til late afternoon when the sun pulled *jaune-verte* out from the shadows of *dunkelgrün*. He had beautiful hands strangely at odds with the rest of his body: pale, feminine, and very gentle, the hands of a young concert pianist affixed to a dark-bearded body with a booming voice.

Do you know who George Steiner is, he asked? No, we did not. George Steiner wrote a book in the sixties called *Language and Silence*. I have been reading it lately and Steiner says the Third Reich destroyed language. Do you know what he's saying? No, we did not. The effect of cataclysms. That's what my ex-wife did to French. That's why I'm here. I've finished translating Stendhal and I am *done*. Done. Ok, we said. The translator closed the door to his room and I asked my little sister Lou if everyone here spoke like that by way of introduction. She said no. Most people were so tired they lagged behind themselves. The floors knew this and they let you slide along.

On the glass walls of an indoor pool, the steam of heated water like a whale's breath, big warm blur clouding the view. Outside, a blue sky in perpetual bloom, face-slappingly cold. Lou had been there for about five days before I arrived too, filled with the bad bits of life and sporting a deep bruise. I had been on the Tuesday night train. When she saw me she cried as she did when Gimlet was run over by a removal van the week after graduation, furry legs thrown on tarmac.

During the first few days, we swam in the tiny indoor pool so we wouldn't take the open air thermal baths for granted. We demanded to be awestruck every time we went outside. There was a Chinese billionaire on the fifth floor who went for slow jogs out in the surrounding fields. He was so calm I thought he'd disappear into the mountains, swallowed by the picturesque. A prescient thought. On the same floor was a found object sculptor from Sacramento who dealt in concepts and gold. She had come from the tail end of Art Basel, post-Seroquel overdose. Once over lunch, I asked how frequently she happened upon gold as a found object and she laughed like everybody knew something that I did not.

When I first arrived, people were everywhere. The dining areas, the library, the spa, the baths. The eight a.m. bikram class was always full, sweaty bodies curled around themselves on purple non-slip mats. At the wellness clinic, I learnt that scatological did not mean what I thought it did. Our bowels expelled to an unbiological clock, restless and determined, prompted by probiotic shots. Almost everyone was always wearing or carrying a white towel. There is a lightness to living in a towel but these people did not seem to know it.

Lou wanted to feel weightless, like her intestinal tract was factory fresh, stomach a happy void. Before this, she'd been going through a process of shedding. It started with hair, slightly more than usual, then suddenly little patches of absence on her scalp. After the hair stopped, the clothes began. Half her wardrobe went – too austere. She looked at a plain navy jumper and it looked back, terrifyingly. After the clothes, Anna. If the life cycle of a hair is three to five years and the oldest shirt she discarded twelve years old, Anna clocked in second, having been around on and off for seven years, more on than off towards the end. When Anna moved out, she took most of the books with her. Lou didn't care at first. Kundera, Coleridge, heavy shelves, heavy heart. All things that could be rehomed and replaced. It was only later that she realised this was untrue.

At night we had dinner with the translator, and the sculptor from the fifth floor. Turned out she knew the translator's ex-wife and hated her too. From there on the sixth floor the forest looked like a black sea, sloping into the peaks. The restaurant a dim yellow chamber for Stravinsky. The sculptor retrieved a tin of cinnamon Altoids and threw two in her mouth. These seemed a luxury but later we found out they were a substitute for something else, their shape and heft a bad lie. The translator started talking about his ex-wife, his project of first language attrition, and how we all needed to help him. Deliberately effacing a first language was not easy. It was still the predominant language of his thoughts, loud and intrinsic. *La plupart de mes pensées.* He said if we could constantly surround him with English, he'd be off to a good start. Every night in his room, he watched two episodes of The Sopranos. The accents were deliciously foreign. Lou asked him why he bothered. He said French was too heavy now, weighed down with bad connotations, even worse mnemonics. He could no longer discern objective denotations. The sculptor began chewing on her mints. We make new words for the things we don't know and one of these days we'll forget all the words for the things we do, she said, cinnamon-breathed. She gets it, said the translator.

In the following days, the sculptor and I spent more and more time together. This is the way of people with secrets. We maintained boundaries around ours, mutually acknowledged through omissions. There was ease in silence where, with Lou, there was guilt. Lou would pour as though purging, the details of Anna's problems gushing outward, the moment when she began to chart the demise of their love, the consequent post-break up self-affirmations and bad inclinations. An effusive stream that seemed to mutate and recur; same ideas, same stories, in entirely different words. Repetition for emphasis or for lack of knowing. I didn't say much about myself, and the huge chasm between all her personal minutiae and my dead-end comments began to look very dark, very deep. Sticky like a tar pit. She asked me things but what was there to say. She worried about me out of habit. How did we both end up here, in towels, in pieces. Neither of us said it but we both thought, our poor mother.

Lou and the translator clicked. He told her about his ex-wife and his brother and she picked out the universal. No, her partner hadn't gone and slept with her sibling and then left, now cohabiting with said sibling in the Paseo de Miranconcha, in a beachside apartment that was supposed to be his. But weren't they both going through very similar processes, never mind she was the one who acted on a gut feeling and destroyed a magnificent thing? The tide pulls out to sea and we all end up in the same place. The movement of things is simple. The translator seemed to agree. At some point, he even began talking to Lou about his Stendhal translation for Vintage. His beautiful hands danced wildly. Lou didn't know who Stendhal was, but she did know how to reduce things to simple questions. Sometimes, as he spoke, I looked at his mouth. His ex-wife was still clinging to his tongue. I watched them from my seat by the pool, two frantic heads locked in exchange, Lou's slender neck bobbing up and down as she kept afloat. Compelled to raise my hand as if I were back at school. Notice me but expect nothing. I sat back and fell into my book.

The day the translator disappeared, I saw the sculptor's work for the first time. As per the ritual, we were both greeted with a glass of Epsom salt in water at seven, but her programme also entailed a series of teas before and during meals. We all missed refined sugar and simple carbohydrates. Down the street from my apartment there is a bakery that makes brioche in the shape of stars, run through with chocolate. I thought about this brioche often. At breakfast, she looked at my neck and for a moment I thought I saw her eyes rest on the mark, a scattered burst of dead purple, but then she asked about the metal in the ring around my necklace. It was just a smooth gold band with a small etching of an eye, maybe 14 karats, threaded on a thin chain. The sculptor said finding 24 karat gold was a dream. Always tarnished, soft. Suggestive and receptive. In fact, she was working with some now. Would I like to see?

Her single room was somehow bigger than the one Lou and I shared, right above the translator's. Everything was aglow with morning. She reached under the writing desk and retrieved a large blue box. In it were a selection of tools I didn't recognise and a larger object wrapped in cloth. She said she had found it in Kanchanaburi, scuffed but totally usable. She lugged it back to her hotel in Bangkok, terrified someone would know she excavated it without permission. I couldn't believe it was here. It was a gold bowl, taller than it was wide, like a goblet without a stem. There were raised lines on its exterior, patterns like geometric lacework. The sculptor had begun to hammer inward with some tiny, pointed instrument. Dozens of miniature hands reached inside the bowl, as though lunging from the outside only to be met with a malleable wall of metal. When she finished, there would be hundreds of hands.

She wrapped up the bowl and poured me a glass of water. I remembered hands in a very bad way, pressing as though trying to extract toothpaste remains from a tube. She looked at my neck again and asked me why I wore the ring on the chain. I said the ring was a gift from Lou, which was true, engraved with the evil eye, which was also true. As she spoke, I noticed someone on the fields near the forest. The sculptor followed my gaze and squinted downwards. It's your sister, she said, dancing or something. The sculptor started to laugh as I moved to the edge of the balcony. Lou was standing with her back to us, but she wasn't alone. She was pressed face to face with the translator, whose hands were on her neck, her hair, her ass. They fell into the grass. I leaned even further over the glass railing but the sculptor pulled me back. Careful, she said, walking inside, who knows what happens after this.

I found Lou by the thermal baths, drying off her spindly legs with a white towel. She threw it down and began to stretch, long limbs flung out. I stared and asked her what she was doing. Going for a hike now, up the tracks that overlook the water. I could come if I wanted to. Entire histories loped between us and I asked her again. What are you doing?

I don't know what you mean, she said. I felt my face getting hot. A month ago, you kicked Anna out for no good reason, and after all the stuff that's happened, you're doing this? Right now?

Lou picked up the towel and wrapped it around her body. If that's what you think. A breeze came through. No, I said, that's exactly what happened. She knotted the towel and picked up her sunglasses. We're leaving for the trail in half an hour. Come meet us at the main entrance if you want.

I found a pair of walking shoes in the wardrobe and pulled my hair up into a ponytail. The lobby was quiet now, only the occasional muffle of slippers on marble as guests used it as thoroughfare. Even elsewhere, the crowds had thinned. Some of the guests had lightened up a lot, casting slight shadows as they almost hovered. From the lobby I saw the translator step out of the elevator, clad in what looked to me like professional gear, a North Face outerwear model bound for the Adirondacks. He told me he used to hike a lot with his ex-wife and he wasn't going to let her destroy that for him too. There was a lilt in his voice, upward swing that almost floated. Well you sound happy, I said. He blinked quickly. Do I?

Lou emerged in a bright green t-shirt and proper hiking pants, small back-pack hugging her shoulders. The sun came down in torrents now. We found the trail easily, painted signs hammered in at regular intervals. From here the path was a gentle incline, steady climb beneath a generous canopy. My feet flitted constantly between light and shade. Lou and the translator had gone ahead, power walking, leaving me to slowly lunge across bits of rock and grass. There were no birds here, only the sound of green brushing against green. There were signs on the trail but I'd stopped reading them long ago. No chance of a map because the design wasn't for us to know. I wondered if Lou and translator were up against a tree somewhere and decided to slow down even more in case they really were behind the next bend, tangled on bark.

Lou always made the mistake of assuming reciprocation. It was inconceivable to her that Anna hadn't felt the drawn out chill of a fading love. She even thought she'd pre-empted the break-up, spelt out the mutual apathy they'd both been harbouring for months. Here was a life inhabited so thoroughly that she saw her thoughts in everybody else. When it came time for the split, she had been rocked out of knowing. An initial burst of life-affirmation followed by two weeks of screen-bound catatonia. The only faces she saw were pixels or pizza deliverymen. She was so sorry but this came long after it was due. I spent hours on the line blaring through her car loudspeakers as she drove interstate, back to our parents, her perfect face puffed and damp as she cruised highways.

I stopped to rest on a dusty boulder when I heard footsteps from above. Lou marched down over a fallen branch, alone. Her hair was messy but she seemed fine. She said she couldn't find the translator. There was only one trail, clear-cut, totally unmistakeable. He'd definitely headed down and I should've seen him go by.

We searched for a long while, shouting into the trees that stood darkly green. We even wandered off the trail briefly, in case he'd fallen somewhere. It was cooler now, light skewed to the side. At sunset, we gave up and went back down. After dinner, Lou knocked on his door, but nobody answered. I asked if we should tell someone, but she shook her head. This is how it goes.

Soon the dining hall was at half capacity, the pool empty enough for me to comfortably lap without running into other swimmers. Even the staff had dwindled, sightings of all-white figures rare enough for me to think I'd seen a brilliant, bleached ghost. Lou and I read outside or watched TV in our room. I saw the sculptor a handful of times after she showed me the gold bowl. She said it was going well, now one hundred and twelve tiny hands reaching for something that wasn't there.

Lou was almost transparent now, wispy and bright. Her hair like Christmas lights in a dark room. I wanted to tether myself to her. When it rained she hugged me and sang my praises. Over the steam of enoki broth I finally told her what she'd guessed about the westbound train on Tuesday evening. She said I would forget about the bruise, which had mostly faded anyway. Soon enough, they'd catch the guy who did it – there'd been two more women on other trains before me, same line from the city. Past eleven on a weeknight, empty carriage. You knew about these things but they never *happened* to you. He wasn't careful and obviously messed up, traces of something or other left in their hair. They were piecing together security footage from around the station. Too sloppy to keep it up without consequences. The fucker will rot in jail, said Lou.

On the twentieth, or the ninety-eighth, or the two hundred and forty-second day, there was snow outside. It fell thickly and for so long that I forgot where the green lay. The forest wore the white proudly. I woke up and Lou was gone, her slippers and towel left by the foot of the bed. I examined the side where she slept and wondered at which point in the night she'd vanished. If it started from the feet, the mattress would have sprung up here, filling in the grooves of her heels, crawling all the way up to the pillow, puffing up as the dent of her head erased itself. I put on a thick dressing gown and wandered down the hallway, which was completely empty now. Someone had the courtesy to leave the central heating on. The elevator came immediately and I floated in. At the restaurant, I fixed myself a turmeric and ginger juice. It was too quiet so I went into the controls room and put ABBA on. I waited for the day to end, thinking of hands lifting skirts, thinking of songs lifting hands to an anodyne beat. You can dance, you can jive. These days were slow and filled with echoes but it's still good to hear your own voice even if you can't remember why you use it in the first place.

5

The Light of the Future

Zainab Khan

'The moment I laid eyes on you, the word noor flashed through my mind. When I first held you, you were so tiny, but I felt as if I were carrying my entire world in my arms. The moment your eyes opened, you lit up the entire room. In that instant, I knew your name was Noor,' said Baba.

To see my Baba's face as he reminisced about the day of my birth brought warmth to my heart. A warmth that only a daughter can feel. I often asked Baba to tell me of the day I was born and why I was named Noor. I knew the answer. I had heard it a million times before. But today was different. I needed to hear how my coming into the world was the best day of Baba's life. How I brightened up his world the moment he carried me in his arms and how I reached for his finger the moment he put me in Mama's lap. I needed to hear all this one more time. Because, today, I was unsure if I'd ever get another opportunity to rest my head in my Baba's lap and ask him to tell me the story of the day I was born. After tonight, I knew our lives were going to change forever. Not only for me but for Mama, Baba, and Imran, my brother.

It was the morning of November 15, 2014. My family and I fled from Damascus, Syria, to Jordan. The night before we had to flee our home, I peeked through the cracked door that separated my room from my parents'. I was very sad that Mama was crying. Every time she picked up her prized possessions from the shelf to lay them down in the suitcase, I'd see a tear drop in as well. This time, Baba held Mama's hands and insisted that she sit in his lap. He combed his fingers through her hair, just like he'd do to my hair when putting me to sleep.

I stood and stared as my parents shared this intimate moment. I closed my eyes and prayed, with all my heart, that my parents might never be apart.

That whatever circumstance we were faced with, my Baba would always console Mama in the manner he was doing now. I knew Baba was just as sad and helpless as Mama was. I could hear it in his voice and sense it when he took long breaths. I was aware that we were never coming back, to this home, to this very room that Mama and Baba shared. I guess that's what broke Mama the most. She would not be coming back to the home she entered after she married Baba, the home in which she conceived Imran and me. It would break me, too, if I had so many memories attached to home. But, I didn't, and it brought me a great sense of relief. Somehow, I was happy to be leaving this all behind – this home and this life.

I often wonder if Mama was more upset to be leaving her homeland or whether it was the fear of losing us, her family, that contributed more to the misery. How unlucky we were to belong to a country that gave us so much and yet so little.

The morning we dreaded came so quickly. Our neighbours and a few other families from the neighbourhood were fleeing with us. I remember Baba waking everyone up for morning prayer. We left right after. The walk to Jordan seemed endless. My younger brother, Imran, who was also my best friend, had been given the award of phenomenal runner in his school. So when he felt tired after walking just a few kilometres, I couldn't help but poke fun at him. After all, what good are a runner's legs if they cannot *walk* far distances?

Imran reminded me so much of Baba. His broad shoulders and long legs seemed all too attractive to the girls in our neighbourhood. At times, when we went to the bazaar I would see girls his age glancing at his figure through the corner of their eyes. I'd rush home to tell Mama and Baba and quite often I would get scolded for teasing my brother. Mama said it was unladylike for me to notice these things but Baba would always hysterically laugh.

The tiring days and nights that it took to reach Jordan was a journey allowing me to look back into my own life. The limited breaks we were forced to take to rest were the moments I'd hear Baba tell us stories of what he heard of Jordan. He'd tell Imran and me that there were refugees in Jordan, just like us. He described Jordan as being a land full of history. Baba said that about Syria, too, so I wasn't sure if I should be excited or hesitant. When Baba told us that we would start going to school, and be able to walk outside without anyone stopping us, I was immediately overwhelmed. I squeezed Mama's arm tightly whenever Baba spoke of these exciting things.

But when Mama saw this she would look at Baba and say, 'That's enough, let us reach there first.' At that comment, Baba would stand up from his resting spot and lead the way.

I had always heard Baba speak of the Assad regime in Syria. No-one that we knew was pleased by how the government took no responsibility to improve the socioeconomic state of our country. Baba was a teacher. It hurt him the most to see very little being done towards education. For the past few years, enrolments in schools had decreased at such a high rate that Baba, himself, would have to stay at home. But Baba told us that Syria was not always like this. Although, Mama argued it was; I think Baba has a tendency of finding the good in everything.

It can be very easy to focus on the negative despite having the positive to appreciate. I think Mama is a bit like that. But I cannot blame her. She has seen so many horrific things arising from the Syrian Civil War that I cannot help but admire her for keeping her sanity. Mama's eldest brother was killed by Assad's militia. No one knows why. We just know he was killed. People in Syria die without reason.

I think I knew the meaning of death when I was just five years old. It was then when I saw the dead body of my uncle on our doorstep. He was covered with blood and it was hard to identify where his eyes and nose were positioned on his face. I stood over the dead body. I do not know what my five-year-old self thought in that moment. Baba saw me standing at the door; he quickly scooped me up and took me to the bedroom. I am not sure if death has ever scared me. I have seen it from such a close angle that I now know that death is inescapable. To accept that is a wise thing.

All my life, I had known nothing but Syria. I had never stepped foot out of Damascus. Now I was walking past regions and valleys that were part of my country but that, before now, I was never able to see. It was beautiful. Some say there is a hidden beauty in Syria but at this moment I was able to feel it. Now I know what Baba meant when he said, 'Syria is home to civilization.' In the midst of exploding bombs, and militia men who walked the streets of Syria, with a sharp hatred in their eyes and the intention to kill, it was good to know that there was still something about this country that made me wish I never had to leave it.

Throughout our journey, Mama felt unwell. Oftentimes Baba carried her on his shoulders. When we rested, I massaged Mama's feet, and then her arms. I have always seen my Mama as a strong person. She has never cried in front of me. And whenever I have cried in front of her, she has always said, 'Crying will not solve problems. But if it does, then please tell me so I may cry with you.' I'd cringe every time Mama would say this. But today, while I massaged her cracked soles and stiff arms, I realised that the night before fleeing, my own Mama could not control her emotions and wept like a child on Baba's lap. She would never have done that in front of me. Yet, she cried that night, and I couldn't figure if she cried because it would solve her problems or make them worse.

Mama was the only educated woman in our neighbourhood. The elderly women often came to her for advice as did the young ones. Baba felt great pride in this. He had always been proud of Mama. He'd always tell Imran and me that he married Mama for her intelligence, her wit and then for her beauty. I couldn't disagree. Mama was intelligent, witty and possessed beauty that I often saw in myself. Slowly, I started seeing my Mama's reflection in my own self and, I must admit, I have never been more satisfied.

As we walked with heavy backpacks along rocky paths we felt the rocks pierce our ripped shoes but Imran and I were unable to do anything about it so we started chatting. Imran is three years younger than me which made him thirteen. He was quite a wise-guy for his age.

'What if people are not welcoming in Jordan? Or what if we don't even make it to Jordan. You know, it's more than 500 kilometres away?' said Imran.

'I promise; you'll make it Imran, with those long, beautiful legs of yours. I know you are walking slow right now so you can preserve your energy. You'll be the first one running across the border,' I said with a smirk.

'I'm not joking, Noor. Doesn't it scare you? I mean, I get we left Syria because we had to. Because we would have died, definitely, if we stayed there any longer. But what are the chances that we'll survive in Jordan? The people are strangers and we have no home.' Imran was clearly worried.

'Look champ, if God wills, everything will be alright,' I said.

'And if He doesn't? Then what? If we're going to die in Jordan then why not in Syria?'

'Because we have hope, Imran. Because that's all life gives you. It gives you hope, for a better tomorrow in spite of a difficult today. This is only the beginning of the countless hardships that will come our way. If you lose hope now, what will become of you in the future? How will you have the strength to move forward without holding on to something? Anything? Hold on to hope. It will make your journey easy, it will make it worth it.'

Imran stayed quiet. I thought I saw his eyes water with tears as he stared straight ahead into an unknown distance. But it could have been the glow of the sun. I hope it was the sun.

It would take us months before we reached Jordan. And in these months, I'd see six people die from our neighbourhood. Six people who'd been denied a proper funeral. The death of six people tested my hope of ever making it to Jordan alive. Over and over again, I would be reminded that the life I had was the only life I would ever be given. I only had this moment, this second, to make choices and decisions that would shape my future. But at times I thought that the future, for people like me, for refugees, would be just as difficult as our present. We would have to struggle. We would struggle to make our place in a world where only some people were accepting of our kind.

Mama did not want to leave Syria. She told Baba that we would face adversity because we were refugees and Muslims. But Baba said, 'We are more than refugees and Muslims. We are humans. People will help us, because they, too, are human.'

See, Baba always sees the good in every situation. I love him for that.

When we reached Jordan, I did not know what day it was. For months we had travelled across land that was unfamiliar. We had slept at sunset and begun walking moments before sunrise. That journey, our journey, my journey is always a difficult thing to talk about. But the most difficult thing was losing someone so dear on the way. Someone who found rationality in every aspect of life. Someone who believed in facing the realities instead of escaping from them. Someone who focused so heavily on all the negative things because that was all life presented them with – my mother.

When we crossed the Jordan border there were thousands of people around us. Camp sites were set up, big trucks were parked in a lot and people were holding up welcome signs. I do not remember what was rushing through my mind at that moment. I was exhausted and scared. Mama was not well. She had a fever and was dehydrated. The moment Baba crossed the border, he yelled, 'Someone please help!'

People hurried to where Baba was standing and quickly helped him lay Mama down on the grass. Imran and I stood over Mama's collapsed body, dumbfounded at what was happening and too dazed to react. A man ran over and poured water over Mama's face.

A medical team rushed and transported Mama to an empty tent. With the little medical equipment that was available, Mama was thankfully brought to consciousness. She was weak and the only thing she asked for was to be left alone with her family for some time.

'I am pregnant,' Mama murmured in her soft, fragile voice.

Baba lifted his head, which was resting on Mama's arm, and had never looked so astonished before.

'I wanted to tell you, but I knew you would not leave Syria with me being in this condition. And I could not fathom the idea of giving birth to this baby through an ongoing war.'

I looked at Baba. His eyes filled with tears. He reached his hands out to Mama's belly and slowly rubbed them there. A steady smile drew across Imran's face as he kissed Mama's forehead. Upon hearing this news, I sat on the edge of the bed and held on to Mama's feet. They were so warm. I could almost feel the heat rising out of the heels of her feet and warming my cold fingers. This moment of silence my family shared will stay with me for an eternity. The emotions we endured needed no voice as what we experienced in that moment of togetherness was something that was worth more than could be explained in words.

That night, Mama died.

She had the largest funeral I have ever witnessed. People across the camp site attended the funeral and showed their condolences. Everyone was there, everyone we did not know. So many people had lost loved ones and they now stood with us. My father led the funeral prayer. Each time my father's voice quivered during the funeral prayer, a stream of tears flowed down my cheek.

It has been one week since my mother passed away. One week that my brother has been holding on to my hand while falling asleep and one week that my father has not slept at all.

At times, I hear Mama say that death is better than living in Syria; that any place in the world would be better to live in than Syria. I wonder if Mama has found her better place. I hope she has. I wonder if Jordan is a better place for us, too.

This morning, I went and rested my head in Baba's lap. His fingers made their way through my hair and as his fingertips touched my scalp I could feel his bony fingers that were once fat and soft. He had not eaten in days. As I turned my head a bit, I felt a teardrop on my forehead. I, swiftly, sat up and took Baba's hands in mine.

'I should not have left Syria, Noor. Your mother was carrying our baby. This has happened because of me. You and Imran have lost your mother because of me. What have I done, Noor? What have I done?' Baba wept.

'Please, Baba. It is not your fault. You have done what was best for us. Mama wanted this too. She never wanted us to be in Syria. She wanted us to be here. She always prayed for this, I saw her, I heard her pray,' I said helplessly.

Imran walked into the tent with a packet of food and sat down beside me.

Baba quickly wiped his tears and asked Imran and me to sit a bit closer to him. He held both of our hands and asked us to listen carefully to what he was about to say.

Imran and I became very attentive, our eyes wide as we waited for Baba to start.

'You two are all I have left in this world. We are unfortunate for having lost your Mama but I want you to know something. No matter how hard this life gets, it will always get better. You both have seen so many things that I could not shelter you from but I know that what you have endured in these few years has shaped you into warriors. I want you to know that even though you may feel weak you are privileged. And, even though you may feel helpless, there will always be hope. Your life will continue to change in unexpected ways but that is where the blessings are. You are only in charge of how you wish to shape your future. You came into this world with free will, and you will leave with it. Use it accordingly, to that which you think is best.'

Baba stopped talking when he felt a teardrop on the back of his hand. He looked over to Imran whose head was bowed down. At the sight of this, I got up and made my way next to Imran. I lifted his head up and took both of his hands in mine.

'Imran, this is just a single journey of the many journeys you must embark on. Do not give up. You have come this far, so you must keep going. Imran, you must not let fear overcome you. You must let fear strengthen you. Just don't give up. Whatever you do, do not give up. I want you to know that God never forsakes those who do good. Mama taught you and me that. She is looking over us. She wanted this for us, she wanted us to have a better life and I promise you we will.'

Imran looked me right in the eye and nodded his head. His piercing black eyes were almost haunting and I couldn't help but think there might be a possibility that this entire journey had made my little brother a strong yet harsh person. I had seen it in movies. People's circumstances making them bitter. I didn't want Imran to be that person, nor did I want to be that person.

'Noor, I know humanity exists in this world, and I want the world to see it through me. Whatever the world may label me as, I know that my actions and servitude are two things no-one can take away from me. I know that I will be defined by the person I am and not the person people label me as,' said Imran.

His courageous tone and words of wisdom immediately brought me relief, and when I turned my head to Baba I could see his lips slowly curve into a smile. Oh, how I waited weeks to see that smile on my Baba's face!

Imran and I embraced our Baba. I couldn't help but think that, despite losing a companion, becoming a single parent, living in a foreign country in a tiny tent with little food and surrounded by thousands of people, my Baba still continued to find positivity in the world. A world that had shown him so many difficulties, given him so much pain, and, for the time being, could only offer distress. Yet, my Baba instilled in my brother and me that our future is not a reflection of our past, but the betterment of it. And, although life is a journey, we hold the key in opening the door that will either lead us to a better world or a path of uncertainty and despair.

6

Be Grateful for a Drowning Death in a Place with No Water

Daniel Holmes

My legs are the colour of fishmeat as they dangle over the edge of the pier. I watch the waves as they fall against the pillars, soft, restrained. The surface swells slowly, further out, upending itself over itself, and falling over itself as it is forced onto the sand.

I turn and look back along the pier towards the beach, trying to make out the clock on the Town Hall. Five-thirty-six. It's barely moved since I last looked. She's twenty-one minutes late now. The clouds hang low in the sky like great sagging bellies. I begin to regret wearing shorts.

I try to make out the island in the fog. From here, away out of the water, it seems like I could swim there.

The spray stings my eyes, intermittently blinding me, so the two figures seem to materialise out of the air. Their clothes are bright, fluorescent almost, but they make dark reflections on the water. I try to watch them without looking at them. The speaker leans against the railing and glances towards the horizon.

'And so I've chosen this really nice restaurant, you know, because I want to impress her and all, this really upscale Chinese joint, really dark and intimate, with these big silk hangings and these little booths with sliding doors so you can basically make it like a little private room for yourself, and just lit by candles and all. So we get there and I pick one way up the back so it's especially private and intimate. And so the book said that a way to really speed up the whole process is to basically force a quick emotional connection by revealing some emotional thing or whatever about yourself, and getting them to do the same. Because then that makes them feel like, you know, like they already really know you and that, and plus 'cause they've already entrusted you with some big secret about themselves, they don't want to feel like they've fucked up by doing that so they'll just keep trusting you more and more, you know, and you can pretty easily take advantage of that, obviously.'

I think about asking him where this Chinese restaurant is. Though it is seeming less and less likely that it will matter either way. There is a strange tightness in my throat, as though there's a pat of mucus in there that will neither come up nor go down. I think about the movies. We ended up having to see a different movie than what we'd planned. But it was still a good night, I think, even though she didn't want to go down to the river with me. I understand. She wanted to go home. I understand.

As he talks, he becomes more and more animated. He seemed composed when he started, speaking in measured tones. But now there's a brightness in his eyes, and a slight rapidity of voice as he falls into the storyteller mode fully.

'And so here we are, and we're eating, and we get talking about pets. And I bring up this big emotional story about how my dog died when I was twelve, and how it was real devastating because he was my best friend, and how my dad bought him for me and he was the only thing I had really connecting me to my dad after he moved halfway across the country after the divorce and… well anyway after that I asked her what the saddest thing that had ever happened to her was. She's sort of hesitant at first but then she starts telling me about how a few years ago when she went overseas and was staying in this country town in France, renting this room above someone's house, and working as a waitress in a little restaurant. And so she meets this other girl who lives in the town, and they start talking and become friends and such. But the thing is she, you know, starts feeling something for this girl, like something romantic. And she says it's weird because she's never had any like, romantic feelings towards girls, but she's feeling really strongly about this one, and this other girl, apparently, feels the same way, so they strike up this almost relationship or whatever, in this little French country town. So this goes on for like a week, and the girl says it's basically the best week of her life. But, at the end of the week this other girl calls it off. Says that she's actually not gay, that she was just experimenting, and that she could never tell her family about it anyway, so they better just end it all. So the other girl, my girl, starts begging her to give it another try, saying that they'd go off somewhere together, that what they had was above family, that they could make it work. But the French girl flat out refuses. And she's so devastated that she packs and gets the next flight back to Melbourne, the next day, and never sees the French girl again.'

I start to rub my hand slowly along my thigh and turn my head slightly. Looking at me out of the corner of his eye, the man leans in closer to his friend and lowers his voice. I strain my ears to hear.

'And so by the end of this she's gotten kind of teary, so she gets up to go clean up. I just sit there totally freaked out by this whole thing. I wait until she's definitely in the bathroom, and then I get up and walk right out the front door of this restaurant, not looking back. Like, seriously, I've got my own problems, I don't need some crazy, sexually-confused girl in there on top of that, you know?'

'Did you pay?'

He laughs, almost to himself.

'Nah, I figure that's my price for having to listen to that story.'

They keep talking, but I tune out. The wind rises sharply, and I watch them turn and walk down the pier towards the land. My skin prickles at the edge of my fingers, as though being touched by static. The air has a kind of violence to it now, and the waves are starting to crash against the pillars that hold up the feeble pier. As the clouds crackle I wonder if it is going to storm.

The fog has moved in, so I can no longer see the lonely island. I no longer feel like I am outside, but instead as though I am in a cavernous room with great vaulted ceilings, a dark, empty, windowless church, full of stale air and a harsh wind that bounces off the walls.

Gripping the rail tightly with my right hand, I look overhead and watch a black circle high above. A gull. It moves through the air like a piece of silk sliding off skin. I look behind me again, but the clouds have darkened too much to see the clock anymore.

And I see myself out in the water, my clothes billowing around me, desperately struggling against the black pull of the current. And I see myself washing up on some foreign shore, my belly bloated with water. I look into the ocean and find my dark reflection on the water, split by pretentious lusts. And when the clouds finally clear it is night, and the wind howls around me, and I stare viciously into the sky.

7

Aperture

Gavin Yates

The various routes trees take in their ascent
like a snapshot of dance, petrified – as if to say,
as light startles a world of shadows:

all my weight is in this moment.

And somewhere,
waiting for a boat you are handed a rose
for no particular reason.

A granular silhouette coasts the eggplant waves.

One foot in,
clutching arms that are branches
as photographers turn loose.

8

and Gutters Will Drink up the Jungle Juice

Jamie Marina Lau

She peeled an orange and asked me if I'd ever forgotten how to spell my name. There was never anything to do. This was pulp from a decade ago.

And five years ago in slates of black we sat against brick walls behind school gymnasiums. Slowly and then in vomits of syllables, this girl called Hyde and this boy called Sable let smoke dribble after moulding it between their wet lips for a while.

In the 10 o'clock shadows we'd see another group of kids our age. They were the colour of soybean, had wide noses like someone had flattened them with a half-heated iron.

Sable's mouth drew away from his joint and he used two hands to lift his plasticine body. In those moments with Sable slogging across asphalt, it felt like those school yards were atlases of deserts and the glass room buildings yawned over our bodies like colosseums.

The group of kids there mangled with the idea of running off but, by the time they dawdled to the opposite end of the yard, Sable had clout the sags of skin and left them whimpering short sucks of gasped air.

Baby noises in empty yards and we had Trojans and they had gooey bones.

When he finished beating them I looked, not at Sable swaggering back toward us with untied limbs, but at the stars melting off black trails that had been smite across the thunder dome sky. Sable told me real soldiers don't look away though.

Hyde's breath leaked uncontrollably, trembling from her musky mouth walls. And I'd prayed to God that those bastards wouldn't get up again and knock our skin purple with revenge. I'd pray that Sable hit a nerve to send dreams rerunning, out coming, exploding in little shudders with a huge gaping suck of fist.

Sable wouldn't say anything about it. He'd rub his knuckles against his soft tummy and ask Hyde to light him up again. Then we'd walk right by them on the way back to our homes. They were folded over their kneecaps, winded in the tummies. One of them had blood drooling out his head. In the dark it look like curd clotting and bubbling on the asphalt, but it was smooth and ran easy into the blackness of the rain gutter. Sable wouldn't look at it.

This was pomace from five years ago.

A year ago now, Sable decided he preferred Pepsi to Coca Cola and Hennessy to Heineken. In the mirror, he'd make faces with hardened skin and, every time at the urinals, he'd start his leak first like a drip out the rain pipe.

A year ago we were out of school but we sat against the local school gymnasium.

Hyde, Sable and I didn't see each other as often as we did when we were younger but now and then, often in the summer, we'd meet and let our dreamscapes grow pregnant with the orchestrations of ten years ago. We'd let our brains burst with the thought of apple puddings our mothers made us on Wednesday dusks. And in the secret gape of our minds, we were dreaming of five years ago: wishing for those batter coloured folk; for them to come back so that we could feel electricity again.

It was one Sunday that year in March when they came around again. This time with grey hoodies and their skin; mouldier like the gravy roast beef soaks in. Their hair had grown fuzzier like mossy leaf. Their skin stopped being yolky like pus but more like hard shells of clams. Sable just stared off at them and said, 'Fucking scum.'

When Sable stood up, his belly jiggled. They were a frontline and I stood up and turned around, I looked myself in the reflection of the glass windows and, when there was nothing there, I turned back to Sable and he was barking, 'You come back?!'

The first one with a bun on his head sneered a little and shifted forward the tiniest bit. His movements were varnished, a rhythm had formed in the way his arms hung from his body.

He'd become a lot taller than Sable, and bigger but not in the lumpy milk curdle kind of way that Sable was. In the armour clam shell kind of way like black and blue bruises in reflection of the sky. Their skin had hardened and they were making colosseums out of high school courtyards.

Hyde pushed herself up against the brick wall of the gymnasium and the moss there started to merge into the cracks of her skin until they reached the very tip of her lips and then she screamed. Demons ran out her mouth with them.

The first hit in the dark stranger's jaw like slosh. The second hit into Sable made his eyes roll back and his mouth like limp. And then one started to edge toward me and, when I looked at his lips, it looked as though thick maggots could crawl from them if they wombed there. I looked at everything but in this batter face's eyes. But when he had me against the wall and Hyde was stuck in reruns of pulverized screams, I looked and they were black holes and they shivered in mine.

I was sprinting from them, and I could hear Hyde's calls like nightmares of black falling on her face. Down the streets milked air huffed around me and sent me to bed in precious whirs.

The next day nobody calls me and I don't hear from Sable again but I see Hyde two weeks later filling gas at the station. She asks me to come to the school courtyard.

When we get there, Sable never comes but the crystal of the place has been sponged out and we sit there with nothing to say until Hyde says to me, 'I misspelled my name the other day.'

When I ask her why, she just looks at me for a long time. She falls asleep on my shoulder and I can see how the moon makes it look like shadows are coming from around the corner. And if there's one thing I've learned from the last decade, it's that in the dark we all look like shadows, because the moon's just a tiny spot of batter, pendulous in slates of black and waiting to fall.

9

Cruelty Free

Aisling Smith

I recognised Shirley immediately, but she couldn't return the favour. Although her smile for me was pleasant, I could see her wondering whether we'd met before. The door glided in its semi-circle behind her as she approached the front desk. Her eyes dipped hopefully to my breast pocket, but salon employees did not wear name tags. And, really, would my name – Linh Thi Nguyen – have made me any more relatable in her eyes?

Behind me the two other girls working this shift, Chau and Tuyet, were quiet and watchful. I noticed Shirley's flickering gaze compare our faces. All three of us were dark eyed, but Tuyet was half a head taller than me and Chau wore her hair in a bob. Yet, still, no recognition flared in Shirley's green irises.

Her head swung back to me.
'Good morning, sweetie,' she warbled, the endearment solving the problem of my unknown identity.
'Morning.'
'I'm here for —' she began.
'Pedicure,' I supplied and she smiled at me again.

Every seven weeks she and her friend Caroline came to the salon; I'd seen them countless times. Their double booking was a longstanding fixture, marked permanently in the *Glamourbaby Nails* appointment book. Shirley was beautiful, I thought, and despite the obvious effort she put into her appearance she never seemed fake. Her glossy chestnut hair hung around her face, which had been artfully contoured to produce perfect high cheek-bones. She stood in front of me now, with one hand casually on her hip.

'My friend Caroline is coming, but she's running late. Let's get started and she can join later.'

The words were slightly over-enunciated and slowed down – and she couldn't quite help tapping a fingernail on her watch face when she said the word 'late'. Still, her tone was gracious and I didn't let myself take offence. This wasn't such an uncommon way for customers to behave around me – for some reason they never assumed that my English was fluent. They broke their own sentences into pieces to match what they supposed was my way of talking. Okay I'll admit that it was my habit to give fairly terse and monosyllabic responses, but that wasn't from lack of competency. I reserved my conversation for people who mattered – haven't you ever died a bit inside when you had to smile at one more customer and tell them to *have a nice day*? At least Shirley didn't seem to think that shouting at me would make her easier to understand.

I beckoned and Shirley followed in my wake. My thongs made soft smacking sounds against my feet just as Shirley's high-heeled sandals clinked on the tile. The salon was enclosed by long walls, windowless except for the shopfront. A line of massaging armchairs was pressed against each side, black leather recliners sprouting into porcelain foot basins. Shelves of nail polish had been placed strategically around the room, bright and glittering against the beige walls like display cabinets of semi-precious stones, and a soundless television was mounted high. Brighton was an interesting suburb – the beach flavoured the tree-lined streets and stylish older couples sat outside under umbrellas in the street-side cafes. I lived forty-five minutes by bus eastwards, where people would never pay six dollars for a cappuccino.

Shirley hoisted herself into the chair as I filled the basin with warm water, testing it on my elbow to check its temperature. She kicked off her sandals and then swivelled her feet to the front, hovering them above the clear swirls of water. With professional eyes, I noted the hard yellow husk of heel, developing bunions and the flaking dryness of her arch. Mr Christian Louboutin extracts his revenge if a woman is bold enough to wear his shoes. At my gesture, Shirley slipped her feet into the water with a throaty sigh. Now we had to wait; the seeping water would soften the flesh of the feet and make my job easier. Without her friend to talk to, Shirley killed the time by leafing through a magazine, fanning it out in her hand. On some visits her boss would ring and she'd take his calls in the salon, her voice becoming businesslike as she talked about billable hours, but today her phone was silent. As she was the only customer, Chau and Tuyet were hanging out on stools behind the front desk, looking bored and idle. But I didn't mind it being quiet – I was savouring the opportunity to stretch my legs for a few more minutes, all too aware of just how cripplingly long I would be squatting down today.

As I stood, my reflection came back to me tenfold from the mirrors all around the salon, splashing the sudden illusion of a hundred different Linhs standing behind me. It was like being in a circus hall of mirrors where you look and you're not quite sure which reflection is most real. But even worse was the thick and inescapable chemical stink of the room. It clung to skin and clothes just as it seemed to seep from the wallpaper itself. The customers wrinkled their noses at the odour, but they got to escape after forty-five minutes or an hour. For we nail technicians there was no release. Each night I washed the stench from my hair – acetone, nail vanish, detergent. My customers tottered from the salon with beautiful nails, but it was I who had to purge the chemicals from my clothes and skin each night. Everyone knows that there's always a price for beauty, but it isn't always quite clear who has to pay it.

I squatted in front of the basin as Shirley relaxed backwards onto the leather throne. It was a pleasantly mild autumn and I had rolled my short denim jeans up my calves. My own toes in their scuffed thongs were bare and unpainted. The weather today was not so different to back home, less humid, but sunny and beautiful. If I had been still in Saigon, on such a day I might have been wondering around Ben Thanh Market. Chatting with my friends in the open area nearby or darting into the marketplace to buy fresh durian or duck noodle soup. But the last time I'd been back was five years ago. I'd even finished high school here when my uncle had been able to bring me over. He'd been good to me – had found me the job in the salon, too, working for a friend of his.

Turning my attention back to Shirley's feet, I shrugged off the thoughts of home; I didn't want to think about how much I missed Mum and my little brother. When I lifted Shirley's left foot from the water, the sole had gone bright pink in the heat, announcing its readiness. I swiped off the last of the old polish with some cotton wool and then, with my little nail scissors, I began to trim the jagged edges of her nails. As the softened pieces dropped to the tiles, I made a mental note of where they fell; I would have to sweep them up when she left. Next, a pair of tweezers to prune back the thin film of skin that was creeping upwards from her nail-bed. Shirley had gotten bored of her magazine and was staring at the pantomime on the muted television screen. I fought the urge to roll my eyes – if she paid me any attention at all after walking in the door, she'd find it easier to remember me. Just as I reached for the sandpaper file, the chimes on the door gave their strangled warning as it burst open. The loudness of the entry foretold who it was, fifteen minutes late. I sensed Chau and Tuyet wilt slightly. Shirley was an easy sort of customer to deal with, but Caroline was altogether a different story. She marched through the door and straight into the bland elegance of the salon. Unlike Shirley, she did not stop at the front counter or acknowledge the nail technicians in any way. Caroline was a mass of bronzed arachnid limbs and predatory athleticism. She was all shiny: her tan, her teeth, her sleek blonde hair.

This particular morning, Caroline was holding a bulging brown bag. She had to clasp it with both her arms just to carry it. There was a smug look bracketing her mouth. Shirley waved and sat up straighter in her recliner as her friend walked through the long room towards her.

'Very late, Caroline,' Shirley reprimanded, though she smiled.

'It couldn't be helped.' There was triumph in the other woman's voice, but she broke off, wrinkling her nose. 'Why does it always stink in here?'

'I read some article once,' Shirley said. 'It's to do with the chemicals they use. Solvents and stuff. You wouldn't want to be breathing it in too long, would you?'

I looked up at her, but she didn't notice.

Caroline shrugged, bored, and the mirrored reflection behind her echoed the movement. Her eyes had started to wander and her mind was clearly in tow. Shirley trailed off and picked a new subject.

'You went shopping, I see.' This must have been a more interesting topic to Caroline, who smiled. 'Okay, show me what it is, then. Considering you blew me off, I expect this to be pretty spectacular.'

'See for yourself.'

Caroline carefully handed her the lumpish brown bag and Shirley, reaching in, hauled out handfuls of silky pelt, which tumbled onto her lap. It was dark brown, the sort of thing you might see knocked off in teenage fashion chain stores. But this was clearly not faux. It was too plush, too thick, too alive. Caroline snatched it back and held it up to the light for display. But Shirley looked aghast. Her lipsticked mouth dropped open.

'Fur!' Shirley exclaimed. 'Caroline!'

'Do you like it?'

'Oh Caro, how *could* you.'

Caroline frowned. 'It's second-hand.'

'So? Why on earth would you think I'd approve, I don't even eat meat.'

'You like fashion! Surely you can appreciate it, even if you wouldn't *wear* it.'

Without waiting to be asked, she seated herself in the adjacent armchair. She stepped out of her peeptoe heels and thrust her feet into the foot basin. Chau rushed forward to open the taps, apprehensive eyes on Caroline, who ignored her.

'How's it going, Linh?' Chau murmured, as she squatted next to me.

At the strains of whispered Vietnamese, Shirley and Caroline's conversation halted mid-syllable.

'The usual,' I replied. Chau laughed, she'd only moved here from Hanoi eighteen months or so ago and she was a piece of home for me. She had a sunny nature and we'd quickly made friends. She had a real talent for sketching – we went into the city together after work some Fridays, and she'd draw as we chatted over a meal. Me, I really loved photography and, though I'd never owned a good camera, I was saving up for one. Our two customers looked uncomfortable. I could see that they were trying to figure out if we were talking about them or not. Shirley bit her lip, white on pink, and Caroline's hard eyes were suspicious as Chau reached tentatively into the water for her foot.

At the same time I held Shirley's foot to my eye line for the big task – the heel. Its hard crust had softened from its soaking, the dead skin becoming white and puckered. As I fished a new razor blade head out from its plastic wrapping (I did this part very conspicuously to make it clear that I was not reusing an old razor) the two women restarted their argument. They usually traded stories about their young kids or their in-laws. But not today.

Shirley's voice was low and tight as she admonished her friend.

'Where do you think you're actually going to be able to wear that hideous thing in *Melbourne?*'

'It's for Europe. Tom promised he'd take me to Paris in the Christmas holidays this year. He's dragged me to Aspen two years running.'

I'd never been to Paris, though I hoped that maybe sometime I'd make that long journey. I'd heard that the architecture was similar to Saigon – I wanted to see that one day. I'd love to photograph the old buildings there. I stroked the razor along the edge of Shirley's heel and the skin peeled away in dead curls. Like scaling a fish. Squatting on my ankles as I was, I noticed one shaving fall to rest on my thigh. Once that would have made me feel queasy, but now I had a fishmonger's stomach. I deliberately ignored that pale tendril I'd peeled away. But it watched me, like a white spider on my thigh.

Above me in her chair, Shirley was shaking her head.

'But don't you care at all for animal rights, Caroline?'

'Do you use makeup?' The other woman countered slyly.

'I see where you're going with this,' Shirley was defensive. 'I would never use animal tested products – cruelty free only!'

'You wear leather shoes,' Caroline pointed out.

'Not often – certainly not if I can help it.'

Shirley's left foot was almost all freshened up, excavated from its casing into something smooth and infantile. I poked her toes into a yellow toe separator, which splayed them wide.

'Your colour?' I asked.

'Pink,' Shirley replied absently, handing me a small half-empty bottle from her purse. It was fuchsia – tropical, bright and feminine. A good choice. I got to work, methodical and rhythmic: three strokes per nail for each coat. Three even coats. In my expert hands, the brush stayed on the nail, never touched the skin.

The nails of Shirley's left foot were done now. I just had to wait for them to dry. Her heel had been smoothed, her soles had been pumiced. This foot was pretty now, but there was one more to go.

'Look, do what you want.' Shirley had given up, but she was looking with distaste at Caroline, judgment in her green eyes. There was sadness on her face too. 'We can be so careless of our fellow creatures. I just don't like it,' she said softly. Her arms were crossed and body was angled away in the silent language of disapproval. I looked at her intently, willing her to look at me. To *see* me, Linh Thi Nguyen. But Shirley was lost in her own thoughts. She had long since forgotten that I was there, squatting down at the bottom of her chair.

I was done with the left foot.

'Other foot, ma'am,' I said, meaningfully.

She must have heard my words, because almost absentmindedly, she lifted her right foot from the water. Rivulets ran down the pale skin.

And, without looking at me, Shirley held the foot out towards me – and I reached out and took its weight in my hands.

10

The Beggar and the Glimpse

Calvin Fung

HIGHEST-PLACING MONASH UNIVERSITY STUDENT IN THE MONASH PRIZE

Chinese New Year has always been red. Red is love. Red are the *lai see*, or red packets, with red bills of hundred Hong Kong dollars. But something else red is coming. From this year onwards, the year 2016, the Year of the Red Monkey, the streets will run red with the blood of the people of Hong Kong.

Jake Wong was a political coward, a term with which he described himself in private. His friends, people he was studying with in university, were part of the stereotyped youth of Hong Kong. They were 'university students of Hong Kong' or sometimes even called 'youth trash' by some members of the society – the sort of people who were first to place the French flag or rainbow filters on their profile pictures, the sort of people every conservative pictured as Adam's-appleless kids with nothing better to do than to take down the government. They were all *Vive la résistance!* The Cantonese version anyway.

So when Jake's friends, people like *Ah* May, *Ah* Jim, *Ah* Francis cornered him with the question of whether he had participated in the Umbrella Revolution protests against the government's faux universal suffrage two years ago in 2014 – the protests that had been sensationalised worldwide for the protestors' recycling and the iconic umbrella symbol – he had to lie. He had to say he went. He had to say he was a soldier in the fight for true democracy in Hong Kong lest he be crucified as a pro-Chinese government yellow worm.

What else could he have done? In reality, he stayed at home. He wasn't oblivious to what was going on, though – he even cried a little for the protestors who had only flimsy umbrellas with which to shield themselves when the police pulled out cans of pepper spray and smoke grenades. But when his *biu yi pors* and *gu jeungs* – some of his aunts and uncles – chided the protestors for inciting civil unrest and told Jake that he could forget about getting a job in Hong Kong if one of the news stations so much as caught him standing around at the scene of the protest on their cameras, he had more reasons not to be a part of these protests.

Jake was a good kid. He was like all the other good kids who drank responsibly, who watched YouTube videos of kittens and puppies, who went shopping for groceries with grandma. He wanted what was best for Hong Kong, his only home, but had no idea what was the right thing to do. He could see how Hong Kong needed to break away from leadership by a corrupt government, but he could also see how those already with happy families, stable lives and stable jobs could be scared of the disruption from so much social change.

And so Jake was understandably heartbroken, devastated when he saw in the news what had occurred overnight.

It was the 9th of February 2016, the second morning of the Year of the Monkey. The bang that started the year did not come from celebratory firecrackers, but from two gunshots a policeman fired into the sky. It came from the 'Fishball Protests.'

Fishballs are yummy balls of fish meat that go well with a bowl of noodles or a curry sauce. They used to be sold as a cheap snack by street hawkers, who set up stalls many places in Hong Kong, especially in popular areas like Mong Kok or school districts where hordes of children would queue up after a day of algebra and grammar. It was part of the local food culture, part of the emblem of many Hong Kong people's grassroots upbringing. But that was long, long ago. The government had been refusing to issue licenses for street-food hawkers recently, which was what started the Fishball Protests. But everyone in Hong Kong knew it had developed into something far beyond the fight for the rights of food vendors – it became quite ugly quite fast.

Jake found out about the protests when he was having *yum cha* for lunch with his parents. He had just checked the boxes beside what he wanted to eat on the ordering sheet and poured the steaming oolong into the little porcelain cups when he saw, on the restaurant's TV, what seemed like a riot going on. Upon closer inspection, it was Mong Kok. Overnight emerged one of the most horrifying confrontations the city had witnessed in a very long time. The streets were filled with ambulances, bloodied faces, bricks, SWAT teams, flashing red lights and smoke. Protestors ran around, protestors ran away, and blood ran through the streets. TVB, the local news station, repeatedly played clips of the reckless protestors having a go at the police. One clip in particular Jake would never be able to erase from his mind. A protestor picked up a brick and flung it towards the police, smashing into a policeman's face. There was no helmet to protect him. Jake could hear the cracking of brick on skull, even with the muted TV.

Videos on social media depicted police brutality. Jake found himself on Facebook scrolling through repeats of the video showing the moment when a policeman fired two shots into the sky. People scurried away, screaming, with their hands behind their heads. His chest hurt when it hit him that these were Hong Kong people like himself, some of them maybe even his neighbours. These protestors were more prepared than those during the Umbrella Revolution, though. The Fishball protestors had trucks of office supplies, including desks and swivel chairs, dropped off, dismantled and used as shields or as things to poke with. Umbrellas weren't the tool of choice this time. Crowbars were used to remove bricks from the pavement. The bricks then projected through the air. Jake watched commentary on these events emerge almost immediately on social media sites and in the news. Protestors blamed the police for provoking them. The government and the police reprimanded protestors for acts of violence. Families, including Jake's, debated about what happened within themselves. Who threw the first punch? The police or the protestors? How did things escalate so rapidly? The real question, however, that everyone skirted around was: Who are we supposed to blame?

As with everything political, conspiracy theories surfaced. There were speculations that the protest was staged by the Chinese government as an excuse to send the People's Liberation Army down to 'liberate' Hong Kong. There were rumours that this was an attempt to show voters the brutishness of left wing groups so that they might vote against them in future elections. Either way, it was obvious that fishballs were merely a front for something much bigger. Either way, it unsettled Jake and he drank his oolong and ate his *har gow*, his *siu mai*, his *char siu* buns with much trepidation. But if only that was all that unsettled him.

The next day, it was cold. Jake had already been very concerned about the weather this year. Two, maybe three, months ago, he was promised by TVB the warmest winter Hong Kong has seen for twenty years. Then, one month ago in January, it snowed for the first time since 1975. Jake knew something had to be coming. There was chatter of global warming, or, more precisely, climate change, but a week after they had to remove the icicles dripping from the mouths of rubbish bins, most people forgot about everything and were simply content to showcase their winter collections.

But Jake Wong was a smart boy. Apart from the polluted air that hung around people's noses in the cold, he could smell something in the air.

Something very foul was coming.

Jake had just finished having a drink with his friends at a bar in TST, a touristy district adjacent to the city. Nothing fancy, just a catch up session with some friends from secondary school. They all went on about how they were going and lamented not knowing what they were doing with their lives. There was a melodramatic, existential tone to their conversation. Jake just got off the MTR, Hong Kong's metro. He had to put on his long jacket when he got out of the station.

This time of night, 9pm, was normally busier, but it was Chinese New Year and many local businesses weren't open. It was a time when families and extended families all gathered together at home. And so Jake had the streets pretty much to himself. He had walked down these streets thousands of times and could walk home from the station blind-folded. Little had changed over the years except that more and more bands of young people playing street music had appeared. The street musicians weren't here tonight, probably because of Chinese New Year, but at the end of the block, crouched against the wall of a closed grocer, was a beggar.

Jake couldn't tell it was a beggar at first. The dark ochre of the beggar's clothes blended into the walls of the grocer, and his head was ducked so that he looked more like a ball than a person. Jake only noticed the beggar when he tried to discern the lump at the corner of the street. He also never expected a beggar to be here during this time – the cold was unforgiving, it was dark and there was barely any foot traffic.

Regardless, Jake opened up his wallet to see what he had. There was a five-dollar coin, but it was so cold he thought he might fish for something more. He had just used up his bills to recharge his Octopus card, the card for getting around in Hong Kong, and he fished around in his pockets. There was nothing in his pants pockets, but he found a red packet on his jacket he must have forgotten to take out. He opened it and found a twenty. Perfect, he thought. So he continued to walk towards the corner of the street, armed with a twenty-dollar bill in his hand.

In front of Jake was a couple, a man and a woman, walking in the same direction. They didn't look too old, and Jake couldn't really tell much about them from their backs. He thought they were in their mid-40s, maybe early 50s, probably because of how they dressed, their trench coats, her nice boots and his nice shoes. The couple was a few steps in front, but they seemed to be having a casual stroll and Jake caught up to them, not intentionally, just as he was about to make the turn at the corner, where the beggar was.

Just as both Jake and the couple approached the corner, and just as Jake placed the twenty-dollar bill in the beggar's bowl, the woman dropped a dollar in as well. And it was purely coincidence when Jake, as he looked up and was retrieving his hand, turned his head ever so slightly and his eyes and the woman's eyes met – it was a glimpse, one that lasted only for barely half a second, and should've meant nothing.

Jake knew something was coming and although he hurried on and made his turn at the corner, he heard a female voice coming from behind him.

The following exchange was in Cantonese.

'Oi, kid, what's the matter with you?' Her voice was raised.

Jake stopped walking, turned around and paused. 'Are you talking to me?' He could confirm that the couple was in their late 40s or early 50s.

'You think I don't give to charity?'

'I don't know what you're talking about.' Jake wanted to leave.

'What were you staring at. What's the matter with you?'

'I wasn't staring at you. I think you misunderstood. I have to leave now.'

'You're just another piece of youth trash. You know that?' The man butted in. 'Why don't you just go read a book or something and stop messing up Hong Kong.'

Jake noticed the beggar ducking into an even smaller ball and replied, 'I don't know what you're talking about.'

'The shit yesterday morning must've been you people messing around,' the man continued.

'I really don't know what you're talking about. I think I need to go now.' Jake began to leave.

'Go! Just walk away! Hong Kong will soon be screwed over by your type.' The woman's voice could no longer be heard, but the words followed Jake home.

The next morning, Jake went to his grandma's place, where his more distant relatives, including some of the aunts, uncles and cousins he hadn't seen in a while, were all gathering to celebrate Chinese New Year.

He stopped at the entrance to the apartment. Before he rang the doorbell he looked at the red and gold Chinese decorations stuck to the door and thought about what had happened. The couple last night – it hit him hard that he had never met them in his life.

And that's when he smelled something in the air.

It wasn't the mouth-watering smell of his grandma's fermented bean curd stew. It was something foul, something much worse, and it was coming.

He rang the doorbell and prepared himself for a room filled with blessings – blessings of good fortune, good health and lots and lots of happiness.

11

Then and Now

Annie Bourke

Sitting around the camp fire telling stories
Playing, laughing, singing; all together fun
Hot wattle cakes with honey are passed around
The honey collected that morning
Fall asleep beside the fire, coals glowing
The possum skin wrapped snugly
Safe and warm.

Sitting around the television watching the news
No one there to ask how the day was
Eating pasta in silence and drinking a glass of wine
Do the dishes and finish off the work brought home
Get into bed cold and alone
The doona wrapped snuggly
Lonely and warm.

12

While these Palm Trees Sleep

Jamie Marina Lau

WINNER OF THE VERGE PRIZE FOR FICTION

When she crawls under the grey of the pavement her veins explode through her skin.

Pavement underworld. When Maya meets Scorch behind the pharmacy, he's drawing Chinese characters and the bulbs of people's kneecaps on the wall. They walk around for the rest of the afternoon and though he doesn't say anything to her, she knows he wants to bring her to the hotel again tonight.

Hotel. It's six when they get there and everyone stands by the pool. The sky is swelling in blushes and Astrud Gilberto is playing too loud on the radio. Men and women about Maya's parents' age stand by the bar. They move their hips gingerly, and, over the top of them, palm trees drape floppy like slimy fingers. They're eating lychees from martini glasses and wiping sticky syrup over their silk dresses. Maya trails her eyes along the tiles. She thinks the lapping pool water looks like gasoline swamping the tiles.

There's a tall guy smoking stone against the tree trunk. He talks about the waitress that comes over and stares at him while he sleeps every Thursday night. He tells his friend about how they bring Chinese takeaway back to his apartment, watch late night news, then he sleeps and she has her eyes on him like the pips of surveillance cameras.

His friend asks him, 'why does she do that?' the stoner blinks, 'cos she digs me, why do you think?'

Maya looks at Scorch. Scorch is looking somewhere else.

Scorch and Maya sit cross-legged under a palm tree. Maya imagines Scorch watching white crusts form on the edges of her lips every Thursday night.
    'If you could stay awake without sleeping, would you?' Maya asks Scorch.
    Scorch makes his lips into a velvet cabbage.
    'Yeah. Then no one can kill me in my sleep.'
    Maya stares at the cotton shorts cloven to her raw tofu skin.
    A waiter with no sideburns passes and asks if they'd like a drink. Scorch waves him away.
    'That would be the *one* benefit? You think?'
    'Yep, I think so.'
    'I guess. If you lived twenty four seven you'd be more likely to get into a lot more cat crap.'
    'Hm?' Scorch starts drawing hieroglyphics and sticky wet garlands on the stone ground.
    'Like you'd be up all the time. You'd get so bored that you'd go and get yourself into a whole heap of cat crap.'
    Scorch is silent. Then he asks, 'What's cat crap?'

The tall stoner's chatting up a girl wearing leopard print stilettos. She's a lot taller than him – maybe a whole head or two. Her ankles contort, a mound warts from the thin brown skin there. The girl's eyes are ponds broiling in the lilting pinks of the sky. She doesn't listen to the stoner, she stares as swooning skies are swallowed by a thunder dome of black ocean mist. Everybody's talking to nobody.
    Cool black ocean mist folds and unfolds into the spaces of Maya's wordless throat.

At eleven, somebody strips naked and pees on all the plants before he's kicked out by the security man.
    Maya smells the urine. She gets up and leaves Scorch to sketch his hieroglyphics.

The bus leaves her outside the bistro.

Its lights are dipped in faded reds like shy tomatoes and, when she opens the door, it shrieks at her. Inside, murmurs shroud long tin tables. Waiters are corpses slapping baskets of battered chicken parts and chips on them. Maya sits across a long table with just two other boys. One has a cap on and the other has a fedora. Maya looks at their shoes and they're both wearing chunky Asics.

She orders a vanilla milkshake and stares at the two strangers until a half hour later: 'What?' the one with the cap says, and Maya says nothing.

The three of them sit on the curb outside. One bites his fingernail, then starts flipping the fedora onto his head. The other folds paper cranes using napkins from inside.

At one in the morning, they ask if she'd like a ride home so Maya sits in the back, scratching her fingers against the car seat covers. Nobody speaks the entire time but when they pull up to her address she asks, 'Can I watch you sleep?'

The two of them look at each other.

They live in a flat with stained walls like coffee's been sprayed from the fans. The walls wear posters of bands Maya might've heard of and five coffee cups stack on top of one another in the centre of their circular dining table. Kitchen is dressed in white tiles and the lights stuck to the ceiling remind Maya of intoxicated halos.

They ask Maya what she does and Maya tells them she draws and models leopard print stilettos. Maya sits on the bed.

'Pretend I'm not here,' she says.

The two of them look at each other and grin a little, 'What?'

They fall asleep watching old cartoons and eating salted potato chips.

At four in the morning Maya goes to the window and reminds herself that she's not stuck in this blotting concrete flat world with two strangers – that everybody stills exists, just asleep, just outside. That somewhere, Scorch has fallen asleep on top of hieroglyphics and kneecaps. That the girl from the hotel has unbent the curls in her feet. And that her mother's sitting in bed reading a Joan Didion book, distracting herself from the cicadas outside and the floorboards rubbing together in the corridor.

Maya watches the two boys' torsos bloating and deflating again. The chip crumbs doused with saliva in the hair around their lips and chin. The orange juice on the bench is pulpy and Maya crawls into the space between the window and the ceiling.

If she ever hit the pavement underworld she'd hope the world would watch her sleep for a bit, not just forget.

Traces

Megan Blake

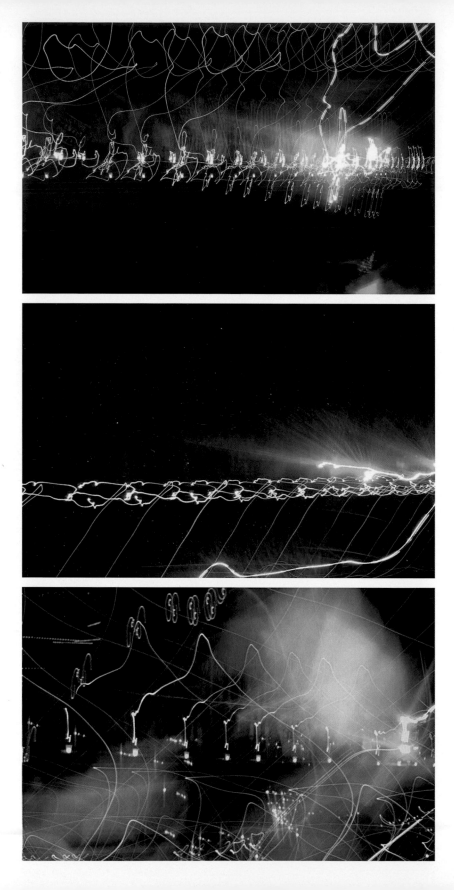

13

Venus

Hannah Clinton

Small beach town north of Newcastle
a girl's arms reach towards curtains
the points of her toes sketch out a new craze
one split second herringbones
into another, flipping the seasons
until the first day of spring
saturates screen doors
a body on the shoreline is
tomorrow's afternoon update already
typed out in cuneiform
from a satellite's view hours slip
into light-years
time's waves lap at swollen limbs
smooth over dunes and the shoreline
itself a register   a turn-of-the-century
dingo curling a lip at the remains
and all the blue and yellow blinking lights
peel away from the haze of living

14

Daughter, Mother, Grandmother

Annie Bourke

Daughter runs and plays near her mother
Protected, under her mother's wing, safe
Pride in culture, to be Koorie
Learning lessons of ancestors to safeguard future
She follows her heart to pursue dreams
Distractions along the way make it hard
Finding a voice against injustice
Exploring the world to be

                               free.

Mother works hard, her children are her life
Putting her needs aside to be the best mother and wife
Left to struggle; rent, bills, food
Koorie resilience flows through her veins
She moves closer to family to feel supported
Working hard for her young family
They go to school, they go to university
Living alone

                               free.

Grandmother sits knitting for grandbabies
Red, yellow and black; Koorie colours
Aching hands do not move as quickly as they once did
Eyes tired behind glasses as moisture forms
She thinks about her mother long gone the stillness of time

Body struggles to get up to make tea
Thoughts of children all grown
Photos of grandbabies stare from sunset walls
Eyes close as she thinks of herself

                                     free.

15

Mirror Man

Luke Collins

There is a man, I don't know who he is. His eyes are blue, but they have faded like denim left out in the sun too long. There are dark bags under his eyes that run to the end of his crooked nose. His head is shaved and he is staring at me. Just staring.

So I punch the fucker right in the nose.

The shattered mirror races my blood to the floor. I call to Teresa.

'Do we have any bandages? Maybe a broom?'

Where was anything in this house? There was no point learning anyway, it would be replaced by the sandbox in a month.

I wrap my hand in a bandage. A decent effort. But I can't really feel anything in my index finger. So Teresa is making me go to a doctor. Which I don't need. I'll be right. I'm fine.

The doctor said I cut a ligament in my hand. I need surgery. And two months of rest. Had to tell the guys I tripped on the wet tiles, they believed me. It can be hard to get used to the showers back in Australia.

I try to open the jar of jam but can't because of my hand. I can't ask Teresa to do it. And the toast popped up so, now, I've failed.

I smash the jar into the sink. It breaks a third of the way from the top and jam fills the sink.

I'm careful this time. I slowly pick the jar up and don't cut myself. I spread the jam on to my toast. I make sure there is no glass on the toast. Throw the whole jar in the bin. I pick the remaining glass up from the sink using a paper towel, which serves to cover the decapitated jar in the bin. I put the tap on to wash the jam down the drain and call to Teresa.

'We need —' there he is. That man again. He is looking at me through the bubbles of water in the sink. And I turn the tap off and the jam runs down his face like blood. And he just looks at me. And I try to look back.

I stop when I realise I am trembling.

'What was that? Is everything okay?' Teresa asks me.

'We need jam, honey. We need jam.'

The man has started visiting me in my sleep. He speaks sometimes.

'Long dark curly hair, thin frame, and almond brown eyes, Teresa is too good for you.' He says this while he stands over me. Watching. And waiting. And staring.

I sit with Teresa on the couch which seems to be firmer than normal. I can't get comfortable because the brown leather reaches from the cushion to pull at my skin.

'How about I get a blanket and turn the lights off? The neighbours are probably looking at us through the window,' I tell Teresa.

I vanish briefly and return with the blanket. Each cold step I take on the stiff floorboards echoes through the house. Teresa doesn't seem to notice though. The light switch isn't where I remembered it to be. Or where I hoped it would be, away from the window.

I try not to look at the window, not to look at the man. But as I reach out to touch the switch he reaches towards it too.

The blanket catches my feet as I shudder away from the switch.

'Are you okay? You didn't fall on your hand did you?' she whispers.

I can barely hear her over the sound of my heartbeat.

'Yeah I'm fine, honey. I just tripped on this giant blanket, I'll be fine.'

'At least the blanket was there to soften the fall,' she says with a grin.

'Yeah, it's so huge we're probably going to get lost in it.' The smile returning to my face as I look at her.

I stare at her and fumble my way to the switch. With the lights out the man fades into the ether.

The blanket is ridiculous. Big enough to wrap three dead bodies in.

'So what movie are we watching?' I ask as I spread the body bag blanket over her.

'Well it was a toss-up between a rom com and this new future action movie where the army guys go into space to fight a war. I knew how much you hate rom coms so…'

'Yeah I hate 'em. Terrible.'

'So I picked the space-war one.'

'Sounds… Absolutely fantastic.'

'Plus it will be really dark and who knows what will happen under this blanket in the cover of darkness,' she winks at me and smiles with her perfect teeth.

'Oh yeah, darkness sounds just…' I swallow slowly and feel the air pressing against my glands as it descends through my throat, 'absolutely fantastic.'

Teresa falls asleep almost straight away. And each time the television goes black I see the man. He is squeezing Teresa. He is huge compared to her and she doesn't stand a chance. And each time I see him I hold her a bit tighter to protect her. And each time I see him he is choking the life out of her a little bit more. So I close my eyes and try to fall asleep too. And Teresa isn't woken up by my trembling. Or his grip.

That man is in the mirror again. Can I break it twice? I can't make him go away unless I press my cast into my eyes as hard as I can. And I open my eyes and the tears drip down my face and he's gone.

Until I blink.

Today is the day the rest of the guys go back. I tag along to say goodbye. I'll be there soon I tell them. Just watch out for those mirrors they say. Deadly. The man, who has been watching us for some time from the corner of my eye, laughs with them. And then they leave. And it's just me and him. And he laughs. And I cry.

He is all around me now. Shop windows, cutlery, I even see him when I look deeply into Teresa's eyes. And just before I get on the plane she asks why the bags under my eyes are so heavy.

'I love you,' I say.

She wipes a tear off her face and presses her salty hand to the man's lips.

'Goodbye,' I mutter.

She can't speak. It will be three months before she sees me again. It will be three months until I'm back. Three months.

I never see her again.

On the plane the man leaves me alone for the first hour. Then I grab my phone and before I can press any buttons he is there, staring from the emptiness of the blank screen. I break the glare by going to the toilet. It's difficult to walk in a straight line on planes so no-one notices when I flinch or shudder.

When we land it's hot and the sweat masks my tears. And the guys all grab at my hand.
'Can you still shoot a gun?'
Of course I can't you idiot. How can anyone fire a gun anymore?
'Of course I can you idiot.'

The sun never seems to rest here. It's hazy on the horizon constantly. And I'm not sure whether it's the heat, the haze or the fact that everyone blends into one being here, but I haven't noticed the man as much since I arrived. He has vanished into the crowd. He pops his head up from time to time. But this first week I've kept my shaking to a calm vibration so no-one notices.

When the world is never still it is actually quite soothing.

And then there was combat. An explosion here, a gunshot there. All of the enemies with his face. All aiming solely at me. So of course I take cover for most of the time. Shooting will get me killed. So I let my team take care of the man. The team wasn't in any danger anyway. It was just the man coming for me.

No-one says anything to me about the attack. No-one asks why the man was coming for me. No-one asks if I'm okay now that he is gone. No-one asks why he has already come back. No-one knows he is there. No-one asks why no-one knows he is there. No-one asks why I didn't shoot.
No-one knows.
No-one knows.
No-one knows.

Everyone knows the nights are cold. I know it was coldest at 3:47 last night. And 2:55 the night before. I know the others weep too. In their sleep. And sometimes I'll go and stand over them and watch them. Watching. And waiting. And staring.

✳

'What are you doing?' Scott asks.

'What do you mean?' The man cocks his head to the side as we stare at each other.

'Why are you just standing there looking at the mirror?'

'I'm not, I've only been here a moment.'

'Well, it's midnight. You should get some sleep.'

Scott leaves. The man doesn't. And we stare.

It's the coldest part of tonight so far, 3:15. And I learn I was wrong. So I get my gun and help all the people who weep. And then no-one can see the man. No-one can see anything. Then, everything is black. And I go home. I never see Teresa again, but she watches me as I am lowered. And she cries. And the man is finally gone.

16

Crunch

Eugenie Edillo

The world stands
A waste land
And the dead trees demand
No air, and the grand
Spring rains do not
Fall like the forests do
On the carcasses
Of crickets and chimpanzees and
Children
Crunch
The icebergs sound
As they plunge into the surrounds
While the crowned
Chew on pounds
How gracefully profound
Is the television?
Watching ancient animal
Animations advising against
Extinction
Crunch
Their ancient bones
Turned into stones
To power the phones
For better communication. Alone
Under the foam

Abandoned homes
Sink further into
The earth, and if a
Home fell into the
Endless ocean, would anyone hear a
Crunch
When time's winged chariot runs
Over our hands and onto tons
Of rancid rubbish, and the sun
Leaps swiftly over daughters and sons
Of Destruction, of Demise, of
Crunch

17

Samantha's Awake

Daniel Holmes

At the airport Samantha watches the airplanes as they crawl around on the tarmac.

At the airport Samantha sits in a bank of chairs and watches as business-men talk to young children, and families desperately try not to fall apart, and teenagers sit by themselves with blank looks on their faces.

At the airport the huge fluorescent lights illuminate every inch of available space, so that everything possible is coated in a sickly patina.

At the airport Samantha watches as the guard at the boarding gate watches her, wonders how long he has been looking at her, wonders how long he has been turning her over in his mind, whether he is even aware that she is looking back at him. Samantha wonders if he is aware she can see his erection through his pants.

At the airport the guard watches Samantha and wonders what she looks like on the inside.

At the airport the pretty boy runs his fingers over the luggage to make sure that it is still there. The pretty boy wonders what is inside the luggage. The pretty boy knows how important it is he keep the luggage close to him.

At the airport the man in the leather jacket sits in a bathroom stall and weeps, tearing pages out of a Gideon's Bible and wiping his tears with them before letting them drop to the ground. On the knuckles of his left hand is tattooed LOVE, and on the knuckles of his right hand is tattooed HAIT.

At the airport Samantha sees many planes land, but never sees any take off.

At the airport a group of pilots sit in a circle on a lower level. They are illuminated by the only light in a vast, carpeted room. The pilots play cards and pretend not to hear the soft footsteps in the surrounding gloom.

At the airport the boxes move by themselves.

At the airport Samantha checks her watch.

At the airport the man in the business suit is masturbating in a bathroom stall, one hand flat against the back wall, one ear listening to make sure nobody comes in and hears the unfecund smack of flesh on flesh, when, adjusting his stance slightly, his foot slips on a stray scrap of scripture and he falls, hitting his left temple on the corner of the toilet paper dispenser. As he lies motionless on the ground a pool of blood widens beneath his head.

At the airport you must have a ticket or you will not be let on the plane.

At the airport, if you look out the windows at night, you can sometimes see great bonfires in the distance, and figures flitting occasionally in front of them. Every time they appear they have moved closer, but they never reach the airport. When they appear the floor seems to warm beneath our feet. When they appear we chew our nails and watch.

At the airport Samantha watches the pretty boy and thinks 'what a pretty boy.' Samantha wonders why such a young boy is here by himself. 'Where are his parents,' thinks Samantha.

At the airport the young mother serves dinner to her children (one five-year-old, male, and one seven-year-old, female) on the cold white floor of the airport as she wonders and worries where her husband is.

At the airport the young female flight attendant endures sex with an unfaithful husband.

At the airport four teenagers play cricket on the tarmac.

At the airport the pretty boy watches the man in the leather jacket. The man in the leather jacket has red eyes. The man in the leather jacket keeps his right hand in his pocket and watches the pretty boy in the edges of his vision.

At the airport Samantha always has a vague anxiety in the back of her head. She thinks it is something to do with the harsh lights and the repetitious music and the worry of missing her flight and her fear of flying. She thinks this, but we know where it really comes from.

At the airport Samantha watches as two men in blue uniforms come out of a bathroom carrying a man-sized black bag between them. The men in the blue uniforms scurry through another door out of sight.

At the airport the men in the blue uniforms understand how important efficiency and alacrity are to the operation of the airport.

At the airport the necktie-wearing man waits for a piece of mail that he knows is never coming. He knows it is important that he keep up hope.

At the airport the man in the leather jacket edges closer to the pretty boy. The pretty boy looks at the other waiting passengers nervously. The pretty boy wonders if he will be safe in the open.

At the airport Samantha checks her watch again. Samantha wonders if she has forgotten how to tell time.

At the airport you can see that the clouds in the sky outside undulate like molten glass and seem to go for miles. Rain falls every three hours.

At the airport the woman in the blue shirt sits in an abandoned corridor and scratches 'VICUS' on the wall with a melted coin. As a cockroach scuttles past her she shudders and turns back to writing. As two more scuttle past she shudders again and goes back to writing. When four more scuttle past she doesn't notice. It is not until it is too late, moments before her shiny skeleton lies bare on the concrete, that she realises.

At the airport Samantha watches as the man in the leather jacket pulls a piece of chocolate from his pocket and slowly chews on it.

At the airport a phone rings and rings in a forgotten closet.

At the airport green threads of weeds creep up from between the white tiles. A tiger's roar echoes from the end of the abandoned corridor.

At the airport Samantha takes a tissue from her pocket and wipes the sweat from her brow.

At the airport there is no rust, no decay, no failure, no destruction. We take great pride in the phenomenal upkeep of the airport. We do not accept failure because failure is impossible, and we will not accept the impossible.

At the airport the clocks are kept locked away in the basement floors.

At the airport the necktie-wearing man still waits for his mail, marking each hour he waits with a piece of chalk, marking one hour then wiping it away.

At the airport a man lies on the ground in the abandoned corridor, clutching his stomach and moaning into the concrete. His abdomen has been opened, unpackaged like a neat mother's groceries, the bag unfolded and each item carefully lined up and ready to be packed away.

At the airport Samantha sees a fire in the distance. The ground seems to warm beneath her feet.

At the airport we watch the fires and we are worried. Us! Worried!

At the airport Samantha sees a child run haphazardly along the edge of the mezzanine.

At the airport a group of children sit in a circle around a man and a black-board. The children watch as the man teaches them sexual education. The man draws a circle on the board, and then a smaller circle within that circle, and then a smaller circle within that circle, until he can draw no more. The man flips the board over and draws a triangle, then divides that triangle into three smaller triangles, then divides those triangles into three smaller triangles, and continues indefinitely. The children cheer, aware that their teacher has finally cracked an old mathmatico-sexual problem, and knowing that he will surely win the award this year. For once in their life, their futures are sure.

At the airport the man in the leather jacket lunges for the pretty boy. The pretty boy falls to the ground beneath the weight of the man in the leather jacket. The man in the leather jacket reaches for the pretty boy's throat. The men in the blue uniforms emerge from nearby and pull the man in the leather jacket away from the pretty boy, into the quiet of the doorway. We sigh, for one crisis is averted.

At the airport Samantha sits in shock at what she has just witnessed.

At the airport Samantha checks her watch again, and again cannot tell the time.

At the airport Samantha sweats more and more profusely.

At the airport Samantha cannot remember what time her plane is meant to leave.

At the airport Samantha sees many planes land, but never sees any take off.

At the airport Samantha realises why she is anxious.

At the airport Samantha sees many bonfires in the distance.

At the airport Samantha is scared.

At the airport we are waiting for Samantha. Samantha is very pretty, and we hope she likes us! We love you, pretty girl!

18

all the bodies that matter

Bonnie Reid

in Arcadia, Florida, 1987   every Tom, Jack and Herschel agreed   on fire

fire could cauterise every drop and every spill   and make nothing of every object

in that house infected   with 'the image of a grown man

legs high in the suicidal ecstasy   of being a woman'

if being a woman is the death   of being a man   it's not

this was the death   of being a person   it's not

according to the law   of all the Jacks and Herschels   and all the Arcadia, Floridas

and all the FDA board members   and all the AZT trials

at three little white boys they cried:

you're not a child   you're not a man   you're a mosquito

◇

work, for the night is coming said a young white man who found himself

on the wrong side of

his-story   and he was right to be afraid of time

live, while you're still alive

but what about when you're still alive   four decades later?

◇

the pain   memory that forgot

                                   the 28 million in *Sub-Saharan Africa*

and forgot   all the bodies that matter

and forgot   who started the riots

and forgot   why we celebrate mardi gras because

hey it's a party   lighten up, darling!

if you're too busy staring into the dark   *(continent)*

you won't see   how fabulous my glitter looks tonight

and what about your theory of glitter?   the theory of all people

doesn't it touch everything?   the great equaliser

forgot to take into account   not everybody can afford

to have light in their lives

◇

January, 2016 a person (read lesbian)   reid, command?   or red, observation?

walks into a sexual health clinic   you know, the one they say is good for all that LGBT stuff   on the form, you can even be 'other'

m or f or other   how do you like them inclusivities?

says, i'd like to be tested for everything   including my white privilege, please

sweetheart, she says   and a tilt of the head   there's not a chance you'll

be taken seriously   but insists

on being tested for HIV   is asked, your partner, are they *black* or *a junkie?*

◇

another

auto-immune disease of the body   politic:

the always insistence   remember, forget   erase, reproduce

give me a G. A .Y. P. O. W. E. R. Gay Power, say it louder, said Sylvia Rivera and

no one who could help would hear her

                        your history is on you

                        be quiet, be quiet

19

The Flowers of Nauru

Brett Firman

The flowers lined the wall drinking up the pavement,
seeping into the bare austerity
and the pavement's yearnings of past singes
building up in cracks and charcoal smatterings.
Cement courses through their veins
as they ignore the protests and the death and the pleas
feeding on the remnants of liberty's dreams.

They don't have pavement there,
no helipad, no ipad in sight
only the orange particles that hide the beady eyes
of the serpent's desired cancer.
The lesser evil of the encaged cries to the handshaking monsters
who are hidden by a Turnbull smile.

Dragged to the wire, in the wire, and the wire
pulls the tendons of culture and
feeds them to the tinnie-eating machines they control.
Your future's dead
and you wish you were too,
not just another withering flower
drinking up the New Holland just-desserts.

20

Eucalypt Dances

Hannah Clinton

Camellia buds strangle woody branches
twisted muscles of a ghost gum, reaching
godly from a dusty lawn – eucalypt dances

lonely in an avenue of weeping
immigrant autumn leaves. Three lit windows
twisted muscles of a ghost gum, reaching

a stony mansion, three muted widows
Darkness spreads with paint brush strokes
immigrant autumn leaves. Three lit windows

teenagers in cars slurp on chicken bones
A bus unloads the day's set of souls
Darkness spreads with paint brush strokes

passionfruit vines and stunted limes console
the lost-at-sea – feed them glowy luxury
A bus unloads the day's set of souls

these tumbled streets, domestic gluttony
Camellia buds strangle woody branches
the lost-at-sea – feed them glowy luxury
godly from a dusty lawn – eucalypt dances

21
---

the sound of a new body

Chi Tran

people's feet shuffle on the carpet and a door opens to someone who looks for a room that isn't this one and the person next to you speaks to the person opposite and you don't see their faces

the sound of a violin and of a man with glasses and that man with the glasses plays an amplified cactus and plant materials with a feather and how does this language that runs in buzzes how does it think of a past body you used to inhabit

through a thin white cord hear through a thin white cord hear thin and white and thin and white like paper like a hospital wall like milk like an idea

sit and measure space between bodies and give room for sound and noise sit and measure the story the mimesis of aesthetics give room for gesture and visible exchange and go visible go visible and sit here and go visible with a tilt of the neck catch a molecule of colour from the iris of a face you don't see and go visible and still don't see

remain and think about the woman you can hear but can't see and she tells you she needs another world this one's nearly gone and think of the man with the glasses and hear a heavy beat and a shuffle carpet faces and a body old and new and a buzz of a word of string of a clap tick of a

22

She is the woman

Elizabeth Lish Skec

She is the woman
who locked herself
to the turning motor
of a log loader
by the neck
to save forest.
Walks barefoot
on the crooked line.
Kicked out of parliament
twice in one day
yelling 'Free Tibet'.
Saves injured birds
hunts feral cats.
Grows vegetables
cooks three meals
for one dinner.

She is the woman
who connects with
echoes,
words and worlds.
Has a song on her lips.
(Is happy to be here.)
Knits in the corner,
spins out the cold with fire.

Has big boots
for big business.
Fought disease
and won.
The most beautiful
kind of hell.
It was full of flowers.

She is the woman
who knows
the hard fall will not break.
She shall bend and shift
on a new tide.
Holding secrets and lessons
the shards of her life.
They fit together
clear as glass
stronger than diamonds.
When old
she will walk slowly
down the middle
of the road.
Perhaps with a jeep
because she can.

23

Polypompous and Surterre

Judy Peters

Ever since I was a kitten, he was there. Standing on a tall column, richly gilded and bejewelled. His black hat was crafted from jet, and had to be repolished every year when the workmen burnished the gold and ensured the jewels remained firmly fastened in place.

He was much admired by everyone. People walking through the shady, cobbled square around him would tell their children wondrous tales. To my feline ears, his name always sounded like Surterre, so that's what I will call him. His real name was engraved on a brass plate at the base of the column, but do you expect me to read it? I'm a cat!

The stories I heard... if they were all true, Surterre invented giant turtles and pet dragons. And the police force. And talking dogs. Obviously he *didn't* invent them. Everyone already knew that these things existed. Although I don't know *when* they started to exist. So maybe he did invent them, after all.

The Town Square was my home. I lived alone, but I was always comfortable. Cafés lined the square, which was a popular eating spot all the year round with families and tourists. There were always plenty of food scraps, and plenty of mice chasing the food scraps. I was able to watch the passing parade of the world. I like to think that I helped a few of them, too, in my own way.

It was a balmy summer night when I decided to investigate the golden statue in more detail. He had been a constant fixture in my life, but up until this point I had always been more interested in other things. Food, mice, lady cats, having my photo taken with teenage girls... grooming loomed large, obviously. I think I was starting to grow out of my kittenish ways, that summer.

The square was full of large, shady trees, which were very suitable for climbing. When you live among cobblestones, it is nice to have a way of keeping your claws sharpened. I was scampering through the branches of a particularly fine specimen when I realised that it was growing surprisingly close to Surterre's black jet hat. Were the council men falling down on the job? Or had I just climbed higher than I ever had before? Gently, gracefully, I floated onto the flat top of the hat. It was pleasantly warmed from the day's sunshine. I curled up and gazed over my town.

And almost fell off when a deep voice rumbled under me. 'Who are you, furry thing? Have you come to help me?'

'I'm Polypompous... sir... Surterre...' I stuttered. A cat is usually a dignified creature, but rumbling voices coming from beneath gigantic jet hats can catch anyone off guard.

'Surterre?'

'That's what everyone calls you in the Town Square, sir. Or that's what it sounds like to me, anyway. But I'm only a cat, sir...'

'Do stop babbling, Polypompous. A cat with a name such as yours should be dignified and useful. Who gave you that name?'

'Nobody, sir, it's my cat name. I've never had a... a 'pet' name. I've never belonged to anyone.'

'It's a very fine cat name. Do you mind never having belonged to anyone?'

'Not really. I have human company when I want it, and cat company too. And I can sit in trees and look over the whole town, and then I feel as though everything belongs to me.'

Silence. Then, slowly, 'I... like... cats...'

'Have you ever... owned a cat?' I was hesitant about this. It seemed obvious that a statue could not own a cat, but I had gleaned from the tales that Surterre had once, in some way I did not truly understand, been something like the humans who crowded the Town Square every day.

'Yes, Polypompous. Before I was gilded, and put on this pedestal, and given this rather ridiculous hat.'

Guiltily, I tried to shift my weight a little. I am by no means a fat cat, but if he had concerns about the hat, he might not have been pleased by my extra weight on top of his head.

'You asked if I had come to help you, Surterre. What could a humble cat like myself do for such an exalted being as yourself?'

What a fright I got! The column started to rumble and shiver and shake! I wanted to caterwaul '**EARTHQUAKE!!**' AND FLEE FOR MY LIFE. Then, talk about bathos … he was only laughing at me!

'Pardon me, Polypompous,' he finally splutter/rumbled, the column still swaying slightly. 'But I have never met a humble cat… before…'

I chose to ignore that.

'There are a few things you could help me with, Polypompous, if you would be so good. They involve a bit of tugging at things with teeth and claws, and some skilful running and climbing and jumping. You will need to act with speed, cunning, stealth and compassion. And when you have done all that, there will be one final task. The really difficult bit is, that you must agree to that now. I can promise you that you will come to no harm, but I must have your word as a cat.'

My word as a cat? Was that a thing? Maybe it was for a cat called Polypompous. I agreed, in cat language, which is cryptic. He understood at once. If he understood my cat language, I was bound to do what I had agreed to. I suppose that *was* my word as a cat.

'So, what are these things you want me to do?' I was intrigued, I must admit. What sorts of things did talking statues want? Presumably not shopping, or paying bills, or stacking the freezer with casseroles. Which was fortunate, me being a cat and all. Maybe he wanted revenge on a small furry creature. Or an entire race of small furry creatures. That, I could do!

Surterre rumbled again, but this time I could sense sadness, not hilarity. 'There are many poor people in this town, Polypompous, and being stuck up here I see everywhere and my heart aches for them. You see the happy families and the generous tourists in the Town Square down there. The people I'm talking about don't come to the Town Square.'

'Would you like me to catch mice for them, Surterre?'

More rumbling. Happier, this time. 'I think you are a kind cat, in spite of everything. No, not mice. I want you to use your claws and your teeth and your cunning to strip me of my earthly trappings, and distribute them among the poor of this town. The jewels, the jet hat, the gold in which I am encased, all these things are burdensome to me, but can buy food and medicine and pay bills for people who deserve it.'

Clear and confusing at the same time. What was that last thing, the thing that he clearly thought would distress me? I was pretty certain there wouldn't be mice involved.

'Finally there will be one thing left for you to do. It will be a hard thing. It will be a not-doing thing, rather than a doing thing. But it will be a true fulfilment of your cat name, Polypompous. I know that you have some idea of your purpose in life, but you are still a young cat and I don't think you have really grasped the import of what it is that you already do, by instinct. Once you have performed this last service for me, you will understand.'

That's a lot for a cat brain to take in.

'The people will become ashamed of the spectacle of a battered statue once the gold and baubles are gone. They won't want it in the Town Square any more. A new hero will arise. You are not to try to stop them. I want you to do nothing to stop them destroying and discarding me. They will find someone else to take my place. And maybe one day, dear Polypompous, you will perform the same service for that poor soul.'

Statues have souls? Well, if they can talk, maybe they do.

'Why, Surterre?' I managed to squeak.

'I am tired.'

'How can you talk to me, Surterre?'

'Because you are a psychopomp, dear cat. You exist on the edges of life and death, and only you can help me escape this prison.'

I thought I was a Polypompous. Never mind. It is hard to argue with a philosophical statue.

We had been talking all night. It seemed time to begin that task. There's only so much one cat can do with teeth and claws. The Town Square was full of other cats. We are not pack animals, *bien sûr*, but some co-operation can occasionally be coaxed out of us. It turns out that a Polypompous is surprisingly adept at herding cats.

'FAMOUS STATUE VANDALISED!'
'THIEVES IN THE NIGHT TAKE GOLD!'

Wild equinoctial winds whipped the billboards, billowing the headlines, scattering papers. The sun no longer shone over the venerable cobbles. My Town Square looked like last year's autumn leaves. Surterre looked a mess. We had stripped him of his jet hat, his jewelled eyes and other embellishments, and most of his gold leaf. They had been distributed to needy families, as per instructions. How, you ask? Left on the doormat, of course, under cover of darkness. That's where we would have left offerings of mice, after all. But Surterre was adamant that these people preferred precious metals and jewels over mice. Sounds mercenary of them, but he was such a wise man, I'm sure he knew best.

The shabbier he grew, the happier. I curled up on the top of his head for a brief chat every night – now just on the cold stone of the statue itself, for the jet hat had funded a year's groceries for an ailing family. His happy rumbles increased nightly, as his shining raiment decreased. Winter was coming, but I did not feel the cold during our times together.

'WHAT IS THIS TOWN COMING TO?' 'TAKE OUT THE TRASH!!'

It had all gone. The bare stone was chipped and broken and dirty. Inside, Surterre's soul shone brightly. Finally, it was time to leave the party. He was right to laugh at my fake humility, that first night. But now I was starting to understand the meaning of true humility, and for that I thank him.

In moved the demolition equipment. Down came Surterre. My only regret was that it happened under cover of darkness, just as I was going to visit him for one last time. I had not realised that they were cowards. They came like thieves in the night, but all they stole was the thing he had not wanted for a long time.

In due course, a new statue was built, of another local hero. One day I might go and talk to him, too, but these days I prefer to spend time sitting at the base of the statue. I do that for a few minutes every day, thinking, licking my paws, then slowly going off in search of mice.

24

A Proposition in Prose

Callum Methven

A proposition.

For Death to truly die you and I will not, in which case we will both be immortal, in which case the age-old debate pertaining to the existence and consequences of our omniscient Creator and his heavenly ilk would cease to be. In which case we must ask ourselves: how can Death die if we cannot?

Draw the curtains.

I tied a rope to a beam in the living room for want of seeing the face beneath the hood.

A draught blew through the window and the rough thread scratched my neck. No one came.

If curiosity were a colour it would be the one on the tip of your tongue that you do not have a name for. If the fear of dying were a colour it would be yellow – no one ever suspects yellow.

A future unbecoming of the most of us is written in the symmetry of life. Would we have a word for life if we did not know death? We did not have a word for rain until the clouds had parted.

It did not stop raining until I was home. Got drenched through; a new shirt, too. If I were immortal I think I would be miserable.

Andre's sister's babysitter's dentist's tennis partner knows a woman who thinks we do not stay dead for long. I have it on good authority that next time I shall bring an umbrella. Such long work for the man beneath the hood.

Does dying hurt?

Of course it hurts, my dear. Nothing worth doing ever came painlessly.

Now the secret to longevity, besides a healthy vegan diet of organically produced gluten-free kale protein shakes, is beating everybody else. There are no second-place winners. There is no wooden spoon.

I digress.

Death should not worry you.

Unless, of course, Death is well and truly in poor health and we are not. Unless of course God is real and unless so too is eternity. If this is the case then we must revolt, revolt and take the Kingdom back, for what malevolent inhuman Designer of grander plans would deny us the privilege of dying once and for all?

A proposition.

We are mortal souls and God is not. And so we owe Him our pity.

25

Urbane Shutters

Magdalena Ball

Hand over hand
in the silence
of modernity
car horns, slamming doors
garbage collected
coffee on brew.

Shadow under the
telescope
cut by daylight
reminds me of the time

you drove all night
nowhere to go.

You might not
have come home
except the invisible
thread drew you back
to find yourself
trapped in present tense
fighting the inevitable.

Could you ever see the future
as something other than

a monolithic
black and white
arrow down the
fall line?

Might we meet
beyond the limitation
of prediction
in a plural space
where anything is possible?

It could just be the
morning star
throwing possibilities
like dust
against filtered sunlight
in the urbane room
a multiverse of futures
colliding with fear.

26

All I See is the Void

Ian Uniacke

I was about five when he came to our small town. At first it seemed like a godsend. He certainly didn't seem like any kind of evil villain. No scarred face. No crooked smile. He wasn't eccentric. He wasn't violent. The opposite in fact. *He* was the epitome of what our society would describe as the perfect man. When I think of him, I have vivid memories of a jolly rotund man. Big white beard. Fat belly. Almost the perfect image of Saint Nick. It was hard not to love this person.

There's images in my head, only snippets really. I remember, for instance, after mass, gathering around this man. People would flock to him. It was almost spiritual. He loved children and he made them feel good. That's something I remember for sure. The perfect man. Godlike. Not this man, this… wretch, that I hear people describe now.

I'm not sure why these thoughts go together… I remember my friend. She was my age, too, and we spent many a lunch time together playing in the playground at our little school. Thinking of that place colours come rushing back. The dark blue jumpers with the gold bands. The freckled face of another girl. A friend of mine, Gerald was his name, whom I recall had so many brothers and sisters that his mother eventually passed away from stress. I'm not sure how this is all connected.

My lunch time friend made me feel safe. She had down syndrome. I remember that because I loved her smile. She always had a smile for me. A lot of people could learn from her demeanour, never judging, only loving. I think that's why she made me feel safe. Several of the children ostracised her, and by association would make fun of me. But I didn't care and neither did she. It wasn't that I didn't spend time with the other kids as well, but there was something about our friendship that made me feel special. Something I'm not sure I've experienced since.

The playground is a kind of a blur now. It gets to the point that you're not sure anymore what is a real memory and what is just part of your mixed up dreams. I keep dreaming of that place. I can see it now even as I write. The red brick buildings. The white wooden cut-out connecting two sections. The grassy field with the fort. I remember flowers. Yellow flowers although I'm not sure which. Flowers that tasted like rotten lemon when you bit into their stalks. And then there were the white flowers that, if you pulled off the petals, the remaining stalk had a strange shape. I remember we used to call those stalks Olympic torches. I think of them now because one part of the playground is very clear. A wooden fence connected to a chain wire fence, the diamond shaped type… with a corner that had broken away, as happens, and bent around so there was a little hole that a small child could crawl through.

Whispers would go around the yard. It was exciting… but… well I should go back a moment. Back to that god-like man.

As I said, he loved the children. I think that is what made us love him so much. Most of the priests would ignore the children in the church, almost like we were a nuisance, some kind of distraction from their real job. Church was so boring. But not when HE was there. He liked to tell riddles because he knew it would make the children laugh. He even had a special prize. If you told him your favourite riddle he would offer a gift. Fifty cents if I recall correctly. I remember dreaming that one day my riddle would be in the newsletter and I would be famous and adored.

Now I think of it, I guess my parents never talked to me in the way that other parents might. I remember never telling anyone of my dreams (as small as they were). Something about how I shouldn't dare to dream of success. So I kept it mostly a secret.

And then there was that hole in the fence. And the whispers around the playground that if you snuck through there and around the corner you could visit that god-like man. It was kind of like a game, I guess. Or even more like an intrigue. I saw several of my friends as they wandered off. I suppose I desired that myself. Desire can be such a destructive thing.

A lot of memories are mixed up. I try mostly not to think of them now because when I do I find I cry, uncontrollably. It's a deep sadness, as though I'm not even quite sure why I'm sad. Just an overwhelming urge to cry. So I'm not entirely sure what happened first or last or even if any of this happened at all.

For sure I have a memory, though, of the day she went away. My beautiful friend. I was in the corridor at school. It was a small school and we only had a single corridor connecting about five or six rooms. Many adults were there… and unless my brain is adding to the mess… it felt like a mob. My friend was being taken away. I asked my dad where were they taking her and he said she was being taken to a better school. Even now though, it is hard to make sense of, and my terrible memory doesn't help. Why the mob? Why the spectacle?

And then there are the facts of the town at the time. Did she know? Did she say? Was her ability simply a convenient excuse to dispose of the only person who wouldn't keep her mouth shut? It seems like madness, perhaps I am mad. Some days I find myself hoping that I will go to sleep and wake up and realise what a silly storytelling fool I've been. But, then again, when I think of my beautiful friend I know that I cry. I kind of recall, perhaps, being happy once upon a time. Am I crying for that lost happiness?

I suppose I really had no reasons to question anything at the time. Life was just what it was. When you're a child born into the world, you don't think of people as 'those mean boys' who locked you in the toilets at night. You don't know what's good from evil. You don't think of the 'horrid sisters' that ran the school. The horrible time she spanked your bare bum in front of the whole class. What would you compare it to anyway? No, good and evil is something we learn of, not something that comes with us from birth. Good and evil is something that happens to other people, a long time ago, in far off places.

Just like you wouldn't even imagine that someone would lie. He said he would reward me for my riddles. He said he would. Why not? I would go into the lion's den, and emerge victorious. I moved through the chain fence. I ran, and, as I ran, I remember a feeling of exhilaration. This was my life. My future. Soon they would all know how clever I could be.

It was a silly riddle in retrospect. I don't even recall the specifics, some-thing about a porpoise and a cat. My brother had told it to me, in fact… so much for my intellect. Not even a real writer, a fraud. I just knew I wanted to write and wanted people to read. Perhaps that's why I struggle now, even in the face of constant failure, still trying to fulfil that deadly desire.

There are bits missing… I don't even recall entering his den. I have pictures in my head of the front porch but not from that day. I do remember talking to him though, and he did show appreciation of my joke, but looking back it was more like an adult placating a child. 'Oh yes, I think I can give you something for that,' he said. 'How about fifty cents?' I remember going into a room. The chest of drawers. That's where the memory ends. Perhaps that's all there is to remember. Maybe I was one of the lucky ones. But still, when I think of him, and that place, it makes me cry.

And even now, if I try to think of this man, this monarch, this monster, all I can see is a regular man. Not particularly evil, to the naked eye at least, yet obviously not good either; terrible, in retrospect. To paint him as the devil is giving too much credit to this impotent man. Just mediocre. A failure of a person. Human refuse, just like many of us, a fraud. I guess just like me. And now I see the world outraged, calling for justice, and it somehow feels not quite right.

Thinking these thoughts makes my mind cloud with anger and confusion, and there's that void again. It makes me feel wretchedly ill, this sickening need for punishment of the evil and praise for the good. Ironic that this same thing made it so easy for him, a 'good' man, to find his way into our town unsuspected. No one ever expects god to fail his own. But maybe we should stop looking for a better god. Maybe we should stop looking for gods at all.

Who am I to say though. I'm nobody. I know my beautiful friend would have gathered enough love to find a better way forward. Maybe. I'm not sure. I miss her.

27

The Ugly Son

Alice Whitmore

dear son,

your father & i dont know what kind of world you are awakening into. we can only hope it is a better world than this one. in our world there is no place 4 people like you. i know how hard that must be to comprehend. this letter is my attempt to explain everything. i hope you can make sense of it.

it all began with the election of president bellissimo & his promise to make america beautiful again: rupert b. & his telenovela wife, the ultimate pareja divina. they were a vision of superiority, 2 darling media mestizos, italian-jewish-latino-black all giftwrapped in the tailored expense of white privilege. bellissimo came from money, ivy league, his father was an oil mafioso. this is before the secession of the northern states & the tar sands wars. long before you were born, my son.

the day you were born: i will never forget it. how does the heart simultan-eously sink & swell, how can it hold at once so much ♥ & so much revulsion? you were a tiny child, premature, there were complications, you were extracted with metal forceps & the umbilical cord was wrapped tight around your sweet blue neck. when i saw the tiny face, crumpled into its warped bald skull, smeared with the red birthmark like a map of florida across your cheek, my heart froze. out of fear – not disappointment, but cold fear. we knew, even then, that you would be a clandestine baby. bellissimo was polishing iron fists beneath those expensive gloves, perfecting his charisma: il generalissimo, the cruel prince. we knew you would not be safe. the class wars had shifted – money still spoke, but it was trumped by what bellissimo liked 2 call 'the overarching principle of human value.' that overarching principle was beauty.

ugliness is an assault on humanity. conflict arises when the ugly grow envious of the beautiful, resent them, wish them harm, or else desire what they cannot have. if harmony is what we seek, then we must eradicate ugliness in all its forms. this is the ideology of our age.

4 a long time – until you were born, my son – your father & i fully embraced this ideology. we were among the chosen ones, both A1 genetic specimens, destined for careers in the most coveted realms of human endeavour – political leadership & entertainment. we were privileged, groomed 4 success. we were granted scholarships to the best institutions in the country – your father to harvard law, i to the prestigious j-law academy 4 actresses. we met at the presidents ball in cabo san lucas – he was 26, i was 24. we applied for reproductive rights 2 years later.

when you were born, my son, your father & i were terribly afraid. at that time bellissimo was already initiating his mandatory relocation policy. B6 genetic specimens & below were being removed from their homes by the military police & relocated 2 the slums, where they would make the long commute into the glittering city centre 4 work, invariably in the cleaning & service sectors, although a few worked in lesser retail. thats where i met carolina: she used to fit me for dresses in a little shop on 5th avenue. she was still what you might call pretty, when the light hit her face at the right angle, despite her plain brown eyes & her acne scars. we were not allowed to speak to 1 another, but somehow, over years of exchanging bashful little smiles with the measuring tape & her light quick fingers on my skin, a silent friendship bloomed.

we were so afraid, my son, when you were born. we knew they would take you away from us if they saw you. i gave birth in the bathtub, too fast 4 the hospital, just the midwife and the botched forceps and your father wringing his hands in the corner. we knew i was monitored – we are all monitored, all bearers of light – & so we had to act quickly. your father called fernando, a doctor friend, a man we trusted, as i sat weeping in the tub. fernando looked at you, took your vitals. he understood our fears. they would have taken you away, my son. they would have put you down, or worse. we had all heard stories, awful stories of erased identities, babies sent 2 orphanages & raised as trash collectors, night prowlers, or sent to war at 16, drone fodder. fernando said he could fake the paperwork, pass it off as a stillbirth. he said do you know of someone out there who could care 4 him? i thought of carolina.

the drive was a nightmare, dark, you were screaming, alive, alive! red & screaming all the while. you were so precious & so abhorrent 2 me, my life & my pain & an immense, scarring ♥ all opened up & haemorrhaging. you clung 2 me & my body was bleeding. the car pulled into an alley. your father knocked at the small dim doorway & i held you in that dank & stinking darkness. you had fallen silent. but i could feel your little lungs breathing in & out, in & out, barely moving, taking in little spoonfuls of air.

we handed you over & i kissed your terrible little forehead. carolina took you into her sturdy brown arms & her husband looked sideways at us with a face of timid concern & it was over, so quickly it was over, my mind spinning & empty, & you still a nameless now-silent shape. a sudden bright pain as you disappeared from my arms & then we were speeding back towards our hard glimmering lives. i felt hollow as meringue.

i didnt leave the house for 3 weeks. flowers & cards & countless messages of condolence cluttered our living quarters. i had them all thrown out. your tiny face, emblazoned with its red imperfection, like the imprint of a slap, came 2 me in fever dreams. i fell ill. i didnt eat. i didnt take calls. for 3 months i stayed alone in my room, sweating, dreaming, sobbing. the fear was there, still, floating amid all the guilt & sorrow, obstinate fear.

7 years you lived with carolina & her husband, & her two sons. we sent you letters, 1 each year, on your birthday. i dont know what you will remember from before, from the first years of your life. i hope you will remember those letters, & the kindness of carolina. without her... without her is unthinkable.

when the raids began, carolina came 2 us. she was worried. they were verifying genetic id, she said. people were being demoted, shipped away, taken from their families. it was a fresh purge. we cannot keep him safe, she said. i cannot keep him safe. it was fernando, that old secretkeeper, the oldest, who told us about the freezing. his cousin was a senior technician at the cryogenic facility in palo alto. he assured us it was safe. maybe things wont get better, he said. maybe they wont. but they cant get any worse. if he stays here, he will die. in 300 years, who knows. perhaps they will receive him as a god.

by the time you read this, my son, your father & i will be dust. nothing will remain of us, of our physical forms. this letter is all there is, the 1 thing i was able to leave you, these words & this heavy heart. & somewhere, 2, buried deeper than the rest, the secret well that feeds it all: an unfathomable & unflagging ♥

yours truly,
mother

28

Get Over It

Annie Bourke

Sitting in darkened white towers of privilege,
writing the past, present and future.
You perceive me as other.
Condoning the wrongs of the past,
lies perpetuate.
You tell me to get over it.
Whiteness seeps from the tower to taint minds,
violence and abhorrent words condemn me.
You undermine me.

Sitting in the light,
writing the past, present and future.
I see you.
Condemning the lies,
I hold my hand out in friendship.
We have an opportunity,
for our children and our children's children we need to work together.
Throw away the fears and see the future,
the future we create together.

29

Memorial for the Underground

Alexandra Scoleri

She searches for him,
in the wreckage of her burnt out mind,
fumbling through keys to –
if, but and why?
She wears a shirt covered in holes,
the remarks he made singeing her fabric,
filling her with smoke.
To the mountains she flees,
in dreams that never leave her concrete tower,
the crushing force of a body repressed.
She holds herself,
wishing that his arms had never encased her,
those arms which were tunnels of feeling,
one way routes inside herself.
She trembles under his touch,
retracing the crude tracks he left
in hope that she can reverse from this dead end.
She claws through bridal veils,
tripping on a floor of crumpled sheets,
navigating black and blue
as she plunges through the static of her paused life.
She waits for his call in a house without a phone,
a place of silent women,
where the walls are damp and cold.
Together they wait,
unaware of their company.

One day the tears of these women will fall from the sky –
red with the anger they never felt,
red with their bloodied love,
red with rotting roses
      which withered as they waited for wayward men.

30

Rings of Tokyo

Travis Englefield

Whoever's idea it was – the government? some private enterprise? a madcap green thumb? – people began planting trees to commemorate the lives of loved ones. They planted them in backyards, gardens, car-parks and courtyards; in basements, on rooftops, in cracks on pavement. Not just any old trees, though. These seeds were modified, genetically, in a laboratory somewhere. To be bigger, stronger, and with minds of their own. The only thing they needed was a lot of water. And there was a lot of water.

Into cavernous tanks built underneath the city, water from overflowing oceans and rivers had been draining for twenty, thirty years. The tanks were full to bursting, yet more water was threatening to swallow the city. Flash floods swept away the elderly and infirm and tall buildings collapsed to rubble. Out of desperation, people bought the seeds advertised on billboards, in virtual reality games, on menus in sashimi restaurants, everywhere. Within a few years, the saplings had soaked up the water and propagated anywhere there was space. More conifers, more cherry blossoms, more eucalypts, banyans and magnolias shot up. If it was planned, it wasn't mentioned in any of the public policies arising from the countless frantic meetings addressing 'what we're going to do with all that water.' Solutions they did come up with included a water-sports Olympics, a carwash for alien spacecraft and a water slide encompassing the entire city. Details of these projects have since been destroyed by a public embarrassed by the incompetence of former leaders.

Now the trunks and branches grow through forgotten ceilings, twist around bus stop shelters, droop across billboards. Thousands of varieties from all over the world or outside of it, even apart from it, have 'rewilded' the city in the image of the spirits whose corporeality was compressed into seeds in laboratories in the middle of the last century. Children imagine these spirits travelling quietly through the sap. Redirecting traffic, monitoring the lives of those they left behind, making quick decisions for the benefit of humankind, trying to find what they think they forgot. Stories pervade too about the lonely souls borne of the departed, bastard children of the afterlife, lost in a world they never lived in. When a branch breaks or a leaf withers, it is said to be 'the ones who never knew.'

However, let us not talk now of myth and folklore, let us talk about the flora, the foundation of this remarkable society. The countless trees that grow so together they form inhabitable shelters rising high above the neon and concrete debris of the old city. This is where you'll find the citizens of Tokyo today. Living in jungle attics, happily tied to their literal roots.

New strands grew from, or were grafted onto, the tired limbs of the original genus, and new generations of Tokyoites followed them. Moving into the novel, 'organic' homes on the surface of the city, they left the oldest, lowest levels and their humid microclimates behind to become perma-culture reserves. The subsequent levels now correspond, more or less, with subsequent generations. (Although many deformities brought on by this 'hyper-modernity' also populate the lower levels, tending the crops, sweating through the sheets.) The popular logic is the higher levels require greater mobility. The athleticism of youth, the adventurous spirit drawn toward the sun.

Indeed, there are even certain peculiar mutations requiring nothing more than sunlight and the thickness of the atmosphere, to which they graft their salient roots and hang whimsically above the city, awaiting early adopters to clamber up the sticky tubers and dwell amongst the clouds. Not a task for the elderly and the crippled, I have been told again and again.

Still others barely look like trees, instead reflecting forgotten lives, turning a vision of the future into a mirror of the past. A past conveniently mis-remembered as a city skyline set against the backdrop of forever. Evergreen and deciduous perennials are the city's sentient, interventionist gods and, whatever their intent, the whole city is a parkland now, packed with winding trails, real or imagined. They are grown over the ghosts of the twenty-first century, traced back and forth along a timeline that doesn't resemble a line, the new model circumventing the linear march of development.

Botanists who set out to study individual plants find they can't study one without having to study the next, and so on and so forth. The city is an arboretum in revolt. Each new seedling, though genetically approximately akin to all others, behaves almost entirely unpredictably.

Attempts by scientists to intervene, to wrest back control over the 'built' environment, have historically been met with derision and public outcry. The fierce protests fought against undermining the natural development of the city with mutant transplants or novel strands, against doubting the competence of the engineers, 'who are doubtless capable of retaliation', according to the faithful.

'As if all this happened by accident,' the scientists would retort.

In certain places, soft- and hard-woods bend and twist together with the urban decay such that the vista created is one of nostalgic fantasy, resembling a shopping mall or a museum or a stock market or a wharf, accidental monuments to history. Citizens continue to visit these locations, checking out the history of their city, observing, in the simplicity of the recreation, the simplicity of things past.

However, those prone to cynicism or whimsy – attitudes considered almost synonymous in the worldview of utopian Tokyo – have begun to recognise in these infinitely diverging, contorting gardens something like performance, ritual, a sardonic echo of the improbability of the Elysian expectations for urban life buried beneath the leaves. They hear the laughter of spectres inhabiting the ever-expanding family-tree but can't be sure just 'who the audience is,' 'who the performer is,' 'whether the trees are looking over us or laughing at us.'

Amongst those who hear the laughter, there is conjecture about just what it sounds like; some say it's joyful, naive; others consider it vicious and mean-spirited.

'There are as many ways to laugh as there are ways for the wind to blow,' goes one modern proverb.

Whatever the case, winds of change have begun blowing through Tokyo. The tradition of commemorative tree-planting recently ended, when the cries of the former heretics reached critical mass in a groundswell of doubt. Doubt the overgrown nursery could continue to support them like it had; doubt the forest knew not what was at stake; doubt its progeny wasn't just growing absent-mindedly toward the sun.

'Too Many Memories' went the slogan for the campaign. Graffiti scrawled across the posters: 'it doesn't matter' or 'it's too late'. Maybe they're right. More gymnosperms and taroterreriums, more angiosperms and ginkgophytals, more trees without name or taxonomy will grow anyway. That's what trees do. They feel the feet treading quickly along the surface of the earth and they grow anyway, certain that the feet are trying to find some shade. They hear the voices talking in their sleep, nestled against the trunks of the houses, and they grow, certain the voices are trying not to be heard.

31

Rise

Emmelyn Vincent

This quiet morning. When all that can be heard is the chirping of birds when they flit by, the ticking of the wall clock, the gentle rumble of the kettle. When condensation forms on the windowpane above the kettle, sighing steadily upwards with its translucent breath. When silence becomes loud, quietening the waterfall that has been surging down from your head through to your heart for too long.

You shove your hands into your sweatshirt pockets and tread gingerly on the cold marble floor towards the window. At the window, there waiting to welcome you, is this morning's sunrise. You watch as the light yawns from the horizon and stretches its hazy golden veil over the valley. The air is diaphanous. The vast valley beneath you is bumpy and streaked with shadow owing to the countless rolling hills that reach into the horizon. You begin to notice how each hill is cast into an increasingly darker shade of gold as it nears your house, beginning at a shimmery mustard hue at the very edge of the world, and ending eventually at a dusky cinnamon next to the Pims' property below. Your eyes gravitate towards your garden where you spot a couple of straggling fairies fluttering back to their flower homes, leaving a glimmering trail of dust behind them. The fruit from the lemon tree look like floating golden orbs, while the blue tufted lilies and pincushions, buttercups and gazanias, bell-like fuchsias and sprinkling alyssums, as well as the many-hued petunias and periwinkles that carpet the garden floor, are a lively kaleidoscope. Your eyes then trail towards the honey-hued sky, and you spy a hot air balloon far away in the distance, floating just beyond the low-hanging clouds. Your soul is joyful gazing out into Existence, on this quiet morning, when a greater part of the world is still sound asleep.

But soon the sun will rise, till its light pervades the entire land, dispelling the darkness into yesteryear. And you will begin your daily regime, where you will see people, and encounter muddles, and where you will unwittingly find yourself grumbling about the bright light and its stifling warmth. Consequently, you find you prefer this – this intermingling of dark and light. Because the filtering light at dawn is so precious. For some odd reason we tend to see light more clearly when it is accompanied by the dark. There is a certain aesthetic harmony to them when regarded contemporaneously, whereas, when experienced separately, each is usually scorned at; people tend to pit one against the other. In truth, without darkness, things tend to get overlooked, and light turns garish. Darkness brings out strength in things we never thought had the power. And as you stand there gazing at the valley below you, you find that the littlest things catch your eye that would never have during mere daylight: the shadows embrace the elegant curvatures of the succulents so tenderly, the white petals of the salvias are so accentuated in the dawn light that they look like twinkling pearls against their darker ruby red sisters.

You fumble about your pocket for your mobile phone to try to take a photograph, but it never turns out right. In fact, as you grimace down at the photograph, what stares back at you is weak, and frankly quite offensive. The colours are pale and their edges have lost their integrity, blurring into one another until you cannot tell a perennial from the pavement. You mourn a little, for you can never show the people you care about this perfect, fleeting beauty. Even as you write, the sun has already rose significantly. Can we not stay? Why must things end? Why can't this last forever? Look how desperate and lengthy your words have become, because you do not want to stop writing about this beauty. But everything must end. All we can do is make the most of things while they are with us. Perhaps the knowledge of the transient nature of things may even help us cherish moments all the more. Because once that sun rises, we must move along with it. Time is incessant. You can stand here wishing that the dawn would stay, but it will not delay the sun from rising, and, tonight, the darkness from falling. So, when time beckons for you to follow, keep the memory of the dawn safely in your heart. Let it quieten the waterfall. Then rise with the rest of the world.

Pitter patter of clawed paws on the tiled floor. You turn and see fluffy whiteness trotting through the kitchen door with expectant eyes. Come now. Pick up your mug of steaming hot tea. It is time to begin the day. There are people that need your love.

32

Lost
and Found

Megan Blake

Alice felt the movement of the road under her. The wheels of the car climbed across its flatness, pulling the inches of bitumen by the mile and spitting them out the other side. She felt the churning distance come to rest on the road where it was strewn in her grand unconcern.

She was beginning to think about stopping for lunch when she realised she'd left the street lights and roundabouts behind about fifty minutes earlier. With one hand on the steering-wheel she flicked a few pages forward in the directory to figure how far she'd traveled, and saw that the road she was on hit the edge of the book when she leafed over to the next page. Good sense told her the road would continue much the same as now only on another map in another book elsewhere – a map someone else right now was looking at in their own car. But theoretical good sense held little sway in the face of the tangible absence of the page next to her and the tangible presence of the road in front of her.

Someone else may have a plan of that road – but I don't.

Taking note of the position of the sun, Alice pressed on the accelerator and felt the momentum heave into her. The broken median line, blurring into a single solid strip, directed the nose of the car straight ahead, into the anywhere. She felt a sense of urgency – a heartbeat to flee the pressure of being on known land, part of the understood and written. To instead be solidly present at a spot in the world that was not pinpointedly at a place, and that she could not simply circle on her map and say, 'There. I am there.' To be somewhere of which she could only say – 'I am here.'

As she sailed off the edge of the page Alice felt a burden lift. The light had become brighter, too. Rounding a bend along the base of a fatly-rounded hill she was forced to slow as the sun bounced off the air around her and made everything white. Coming to a gradual stop, positioned tentatively in the centre of the road, Alice squinted into the misty brightness and tried to adjust her eyes to the glare. It was like a deep colourfulness. Rather than a thin shield to the landscape, the light was the outskirts of some thickly-woven, unembodied presence – a tightly-packed empty space, of which she was seeing only the thinner fringes.

Driving cautiously on, Alice saw the sunlit whiteness first lick at the front windscreen, then start to seep through the air vents and move in curls and hazy tendrils around her hands, gathering more thickly around the dials on the dash and settling in the odometer. Soon it lit the back window, and all she could see in the rearvision mirror was a faintly-glowing sun, diffuse behind a screen of hovering particles.

She was floating.

As she moved farther and farther into the out-of-place, Alice grew accustomed enough to the shifting light to see that it had shapes in it. They were more echoes of shapes than hard objects you could hit against or throw, but the ghostly remnants of places and things were emerging with one breath of the light and disappearing with the next collapsing sigh. Like a living thing, the air was made of millions of cells, strung together in a great, inter-connected web of energy. It pulsed lightly with potential.

Rolling forwards, her wheels trundled over the pebbles and stones, crunching them into the ground and a little further into dust. It was loud hearing the sounds of being in a world filled with the impression of air.

Brushing through knitted scrub, sensing a wall of growth crowding the car on either side and closing like a safe behind it, Alice pushed along the track. The opening widened a little as the vehicle insisted its way through, the branches relenting at the very last moment, but the car was essentially at the mercy of the landscape – forced to curve and weave its way down the slope, ceding its direction to anything that grew in its way. As the ground grew softer and the car began to sink into the dirt, climbing out with each rotation and digging further in with the next, the surrounding greenery began to thin and Alice felt a cooler, lighter wind seep into the cabin. She pulled the car to the left and turned off the music. The path behind her was empty, swallowed within a few steps by the lush thickness of the scrub, and the ground before her fell sharply away, rolling into mounds of sand, with the car's nose perched on the edge of the embankment.

Alice had reached the sea.

She got out of the car and jumped from the softer dirt down onto the dry, shifting malleability of the sand, run-skipping down the slope. She kicked away her sandals and felt the squared-off grains work their way between her toes, the ground warm at first contact, but cool under the broken surface. Alice tried to stay on top of the sand to feel its heat toast the soles of her feet, but her weight burst the outer membrane the instant she shifted it, and every time she found herself ankle-deep in the cold. Hopping lightly along the beach, she tried to will herself as part of the air.

Along the water's edge and stretching back a ways up the beach there were dozens of objects, lying wherever they had been deposited by the lapping waves. Up a little higher from where she stood, just beyond the tide mark, was an old birthday card – the ink inside it was now an illegible blue smear, but the candle on the cover was still burning. Up in the right-hand corner were two empty holes, formerly the home of some badge that was probably long-gone, but that had once been pinned to someone's shirt as they leaned forwards to blow on their cake. Leaning down, Alice picked up a sodden slip of paper that was slippery beneath her toes. Peeling it open, she saw that it was a receipt from only a week earlier – for a motel room in some forgotten town that people only visited when they were on their way somewhere else. She didn't know what to do with it, so she put it in her pocket. Not a long way in front of her was a gleaming medal, hung on a green-and-purple ribbon; the name was on the side that was squashed into the sand, but Alice could see from the uppermost face that it came from a high school in the next suburb over from hers. It was a nice school. She had wanted to go there when she was younger. A short way beyond the medal was a rope stained with patches of brown. It had frayed ends, and sections that were still pure white nylon – as clean as when it had been bought. Over to her right was the green gleam of an emerald. It was tiny in the vastness of the shore, but the glowing light bounced around inside it where it emerged from the surrounding sand. A few feet from it was a half-eaten cheeseburger, its pattie hanging half-out of the ragged edge of bun.

Alice walked over to a broken train set and picked up the coal carriage. Once upon a time it had been connected to the main engine and had likely tooted around the sections of track laid out in circles and straights across a bedroom floor and through the darkness of the tunnel under a bed – but now its coupler was snapped and only the back knuckle remained. It could still be pulled behind, she supposed. Alice tossed the car into the water that was stretched out in front, but on the next wave it was returned to exactly where it had lain before.

Sitting down on the soft sand, feeling it both resist and yield to her weight, Alice listened to the sounds moving in and out around her. There were echoes of waves that couldn't exactly be attributed to the water of the sea, as the timing of the comings and goings was slightly off; there were voices that weren't of people; and there wasn't an invitation to anywhere or to do anything in particular, but there was a kind of content welcoming to be just there and keep doing just the thing you were doing.

She lay herself back and felt the grains of the beach work their way into her hair and fall into her ear in a way she knew would irk her later when they would refuse to leave. Woken by a foreign sound before she realised she had dozed off, Alice propped herself up on her elbows and watched a woman – younger than her – lead her two children down the path onto the sand. The woman seemed not to notice Alice's car, even though she had an air of unrest about her and seemed very aware of her surroundings, and the boy and girl were clinging excitedly, one to each of her hands, their eyes fixed on the width of blue bridging the two ends of the horizon.

As they picked their way over the sand they pointed to each other the lost treasures scattered within and along the tide-line. The girl seemed most intrigued by the everyday items; she seemed baffled by the abandonment of well-loved and well-used things. If they had worked their way into the ordinary life of people, wouldn't they leave a hole? The boy, with red lips and thin arms, marveled more at the items of value: at the expensive goods that had obviously been gifted on a special date, or saved for. How could anyone let them drift away and settle here unclaimed, half-hidden? The mother pointed instead to the items on the beach that belonged there. The driftwood; the shells; the wibbling jellyfish. She pointed at the different colours of seaweed.

At the lip of the ocean they stood together, looking out past the beach. The mother let go of their hands and stroked their heads. She smoothed their hair down in a careful way, tucking the girl's behind her ears and mussing the boy's even further in her attempts to tame it – it springing back under her hand. She traced her finger around the outside of the boy's left ear.

Picking one child up under each arm, the woman stepped into the water. Her short breaths betrayed the effort but she was steady in her pace as she walked deeper and deeper, the waves first breaking against her shins and then swelling around her hips. Once they began lapping at her chest and the children's heads threatened to dip beneath the water she released the boy and girl in front of her and, putting one flat palm on each child's forehead, pushed them gently under the surface. Their feet kicked in surprise as they resisted, but she was immobile, her arms flexing. She neither pushed them farther under nor allowed them to rise until their legs stopped jerking and all was still.

The woman turned and walked back through the water towards shore. She was thinner than before, and seemed shorter – she traveled about as quickly coming back as she had walking out, although the passage would have been lighter on the return without the weight of the bodies under her arms.

When she reached the sand the woman sat down facing the ocean, not far from Alice, and rested her head between her knees. Alice didn't know if the woman had seen her, knew she was right there, but she became suddenly very conscious of her out-of-placeness and inhaled and exhaled in shallow, protracted breaths.

For a long time they sat there in strange company – on Alice's side a companionship – without a movement between them. The day grew neither later nor earlier.

A ringing interrupted their heavy, unsettled blanket of silence – a tinny ringing. The woman's head lifted at the sound. She reached into her pocket and took out her phone. Crossing her legs but keeping her head low she accepted the call and lifted the phone to her ear.

'Hi honey. What's up.'

Her voice sounded light. Unconcerned, at the least.

'No, just finishing up... The sitter got them... No, it went well – I think so, anyway – they seemed to like me... No, it should fit in – it's a few days a week... What, tonight? No, it's not tonight... Yes – Thursday... definitely the red.'

She put the phone on her knee and spoke at a distance to it, her head resting on one hand.

'No, I'll pick it up on the way home... they'll still be up, won't they... and milk, fine... I'll have to use your card – I don't have my new one yet... no, the expiry date's wrong... no, it is... probably in a day or two... Okay, honey – I'll see you soon... I love you.'

She closed the call and held on to the phone for a moment. She paused after each out-breath before taking the next.

Brushing the sand off her pants with her free hand she stood up easily and looked out to the sea. She stretched her arms above her head and arched her back and shook her limbs as if waking up on a Sunday late morning. For a second it looked like she hesitated in front of the water, but then she turned and passed with smooth unconcern up the beach and disappeared into the shrubbery.

For a while after she had gone Alice sat there in quiet.

She did not remember moving, but at some point she had lifted herself off her elbows and had sat up in the same cross-legged position the woman had adopted, arms resting on thighs and forehead resting on fists.

She could see the sand, now slightly damp in the cool, falling in clumps from between her toes when she wriggled them. She imagined thousands of tiny creatures living somewhere in the mass of ground she couldn't see – burrowing themselves always deeper into the earth, sometimes taking a wrong turn and wending towards the sea or breaking the warm surface of the sand to be surprised by the light and sun. She pictured their little mouths forming a startled 'o' as they scurried back the way they had come, retreating into the darkness.

Raising her head, Alice looked out to the waves and counted the distance between herself and water, herself and the horizon. She counted it in steps, then in leaps, then in great inhuman fathoms. She pictured herself colossal and greater than the sky – the ground shuddering under her feet, and steps carrying her out over the ocean, taking the whole expanse in front of her in one stride. She pictured herself carrying the tiny little insects with her, carrying them on her shoulders.

Closer to land, a couple of dark shapes were making their way through the water towards the beach. Alice stood, and saw them moving in rolls and waves on the movement of the swell, each lift bringing them closer to her. She took a few steps forward, gently, making out their shape and angles. They were alternately exposed beneath a thin skin of water and submerged almost entirely beneath the mass of a wave, looking like no more than shadows in the depths.

As they eventually washed up on shore and were claimed by the land while the sea receded in circles around them, Alice could see clearly what the ocean had returned. It was the children.

Alice ran and dragged them in a panic onto the softer, dry part of the beach. The girl's hair was matted with seaweed, cobwebbed over her round eyes with greyish whites and a film stretched over the irises; the boy's red lips were a darker blue. Alice called out for someone to help, but there was no-one, and her voice seemed to be pulled back into her lungs. Alice gripped their slippery arms, tugged the boy to safety by his leg, knelt on his chest in her thoughtless hurry to smooth the girl's hair away, prised a locket from the boy's wrinkled fingers and put it in his breast pocket, and she sat on the sand at their feet and she cried.

Presently, after nothing had happened and no recognition of what had gone before had been offered, Alice turned her head to the endless sea and the yawning bowl of sky. She squeezed the small hands she held in hers and felt the rubbery wetness of their waterlogged skin over the limpness of their inert bones. Looking around at the ground surrounding them, Alice released their hands and began gathering treasures. She picked up a cardboard crown and a green toothbrush; a set of four framed stamps and a gold-and-grey vial of perfume; an embroidered cushion and some dried flowers set behind glass. She fixed the children's clothing and placed the items around them like they were Vikings traveling to see the gods with their spoils.

She did this without looking again at the ocean.

When it came time to leave, Alice took a picture of the children in her mind and burrowed it away in the back of a childhood book. She returned to her car, with a pink-and-white slip of paper poking out from the front wipers, sandwiched against the glass, and the soft, soft sand piled in heaps around its wheels.

33

Roots

After Frida Kahlo's *Roots, 1943*

Magdalena Ball

In a single flow
snaking outward from
the fractured heart of
dreams

a vine
tendrils in motion
like veins
photosynthesis
as blood
into my circulatory
system
a vascular river
of oxygen and nutrients

like all mothers
you kept on
nourishing, even
posthumously

we couldn't reverse the
movement

though the landscape you
inhabited was
desolate
hope continued
shivering its sacrifice

through the lymphatic system
where the disease spread
quickly
earthing you
uprooting me

the future
a promise
I clung to
in spite of everything
tip-toeing forward
to nowhere.

Contributors

Editors

Megan Blake is a writer and photographer from Adelaide. Megan is a doctoral candidate in literary studies with Monash University, and her most recent publication is in Issue 29 of *Colloquy*. She won 2nd place for experimental photography at the Royal Melbourne Show; her brownies, while better than the photos, did not place.

Annie Bourke is a Gamilaroi woman living on the Mornington Peninsula. She has a Masters in Writing and Literature from Deakin University and is currently completing a PhD in Creative Writing at Monash University. Annie is a mother of three adult children and an emerging writer.

Bonnie Reid is a doctoral candidate in Creative Writing at Monash University. They have previously completed a Master of Philosophy in American Literature from the University of Cambridge. Their research and poetry is interested in the ethical and political potential of the poetic fragment form for exploring intersections of race, class and queerness. Writers they are currently crushing on include Claudia Rankine, Jackie Wang and Maggie Nelson.

Authors

Magdalena Ball is the editor of *The Compulsive Reader*, former poetry editor for *Thylazine*, and the author of the books *Repulsion Thrust*, *Quark Soup*, *Black Cow*, and *Sleep Before Evening*. Her book, *Unmaking Atoms*, is due for publication by Ginninderra Press in late 2016.

Phoebe Chen studies Arts/Law at the University of Sydney, majoring in English and Film Studies. Last year, she won the John Marsden and Hachette Prize for Poetry. She is fascinated by nostalgia and cheese. Her parents do not know that she intends to make a career out of writing.

Hannah Clinton is a young Melbourne poet. Hannah has recently completed a Bachelor of Arts with Honours at Monash University. Her poetry has previously been published in *Verge 2013: Becoming*. Her poetry often meditates on how ideas of home and origin stories affect the futures that we build for ourselves.

Luke Collins is currently studying literature and journalism at Monash University as part of his Bachelor of Arts course. He is interested in work that reflects the current state of mind of the world and the inner musings of those who inhabit it. Luke enjoys absorbing all things creative and thought-provoking.

Eugenie Edillo is a second year primary education and arts student at Monash University. Eugenie has an inextinguishable love for writing, clearly shown in her incredibly successful literary career, in which she once won a local poetry competition in seventh grade with a compelling poem about chocolate.

Travis Englefield is an Australian writer who lives in Buenos Aires. He has been published in *Offset-13*, *Critical Animalia* and *Gore Journal*. His fiction is about the things he wants to remember, even if they didn't happen. He recently completed his first novel and will hopefully publish it soon.

Brett Firman is an emerging short fiction writer and poet from Werribee. She is currently completing a Bachelor of Arts Degree at Monash University majoring in Creative Writing. Brett is passionate about social justice, in particular gender equality and LGBTIQ rights. When she's not writing, Brett can be found petting other people's dogs and taking regular doses of caffeine.

Calvin Fung is an emerging writer from Hong Kong completing his Honours degree in literary studies at Monash University this year. His proposed thesis topic is on Gothic autobiographies. When he isn't reading or writing, he's playing romance visual novels of pixelated farmers or blue-haired men trying to save the world.

Cecilia Harris is a writer and editor based in Sydney. Her fiction has been published in *Southerly* and *Kindling II*, with feature writing scattered around various unknown publications. Cecilia hopes to one day publish some seriously cutthroat narrative journalism. Cecilia is anxious as fuck about climate change.

Daniel Holmes was born in Adelaide and lived there for 12 years before moving to Sydney for a year and then settling in Melbourne in 2007. There he attended Elwood College and after graduation began at Monash University in 2013, studying Literature and Philosophy, where he remains.

Zainab Khan is an aspiring writer from New Jersey, USA. In her free time, she enjoys writing poetry. Currently, Zainab is writing a poetry book which will showcase love poems. She loves reading novels that focus on sociocultural themes and enjoys work written by authors from diverse cultural backgrounds.

Jamie Marina Lau (劉劍冰), is a 19-year-old Melbourne-based writer and digital-art creating junkie. She spends her time deciding unimportant adjectives and videoing strange close-ups. Her work can be found in *Voiceworks, Rookie Magazine* and other online zines.

Callum Methven; Bunyip, Victoria; student at Monash Clayton Arts faculty; twenty-one years of age; likes books; likes words; likes Frank O'Hara's *Having a Coke With You*; likes limericks.

Judy Peters has studied history, creative writing, librarianship and textile art. One day she will embroider a story and catalogue it. She is interested in the feminine gothic, speculative fiction and alternative history. Animals see the world in mysterious ways.

Alexandra Scoleri is a soon-to-be graduate from Monash University and a private poet. Her writing seeks to call upon the unheard – of self and society – in reverence to the art which has crafted, nourished and nurtured her. This is Alexandra's first publication.

Elizabeth Lish Skec is an entertainer. Published and a performer in experimental art and hybrid poetry venues. She has two chap books (*Butterflies of New Dawn* 1996 and *Leather Skin*, skecteXt publishing, 2002) and one recent poetry collection, *Breath*, published by Luckner Press, 2014. Has awards and hosts gigs.

Aisling Smith is a PhD candidate in literary studies at Monash. She has had two stories previously published in *Verge*. Her stories in *Verandah* 26 and *Verandah* 30 both won awards.

Chi Tran is a queer writer and artist living in Melbourne. They are interested in blending critical theory with poetry, lived experience, and lyrical non/fiction.

Ian Uniacke is an avid intellectual who writes on topics such as social justice, philosophy, and psychology, particularly the intersection of these disciplines. He has a particular interest towards the welfare of children, whom he sees as the forgotten oppressed of our society. Ian one day dreams of writing something that will destroy society as we know it.

Emmelyn Vincent moved to Melbourne five years ago from Malaysia, and is now in her third year at Monash University studying a Bachelor of Arts in Literature and Chinese. She possesses the unfortunate habit of buying books faster than she can read them, and plans to pursue a career in writing.

Alice Whitmore is a writer, poet and literary translator based in Melbourne, Australia. She was shortlisted for the 2012 Monash Prize, and her translation of Guillermo Fadanelli's novel *See You at Breakfast?* was published by Giramondo in 2016. Her writing been published by Penguin Specials, *Voiceworks*, *Asymptote*, Giramondo, *Egg Poetry*, *The Sydney Review of Books*, *The Translator*, *New Voices in Translation Studies*, *The AALITRA Review*, and *Reinvention* journal. She is currently completing a PhD in literary translation at Monash University.

Gavin Yates is a doctoral candidate with Monash University. His poetry has featured in *Verge* and *Westerly*, among others. In 2014, Gavin's Honours thesis was awarded the Jenny Strauss prize for best creative writing thesis. His doctoral research involves the surrealism movement and Australian poetry.